Plant-Based Diet For Athletes and Bodybuilders

2 Books in 1

The Complete Vegan Bodybuilding Diet Book to Fuel Your Workout, Muscle Growth And Recovery Your Body

By

Joshua King

Table of Contents

PLANT-BASED COOKBOOK FOR ATHLETES

INTRODUCTION 11

CHAPTER 1. WHAT IS A PLANT- BASED DIET? 15
- History of the Plant-based Diet 16

CHAPTER 2. WHAT ARE THE BENEFITS OF A PLANT-BASED DIET? 18

CHAPTER 3. VEGAN VS PLANT-BASED DIET 27
- Benefits of Vegan Diet 27

CHAPTER 4. PLANT-BASED NUTRITION FOR SPORT 30
- Carbs and Fats - What they Are and How they Impact Performance 30
- The Potential of Proteins - Why they're Crucial for Athletes 32
- Plant-Based Besties - The Protein Sources for Maximum Impact 33

CHAPTER 5. THE INCREDIBLE HEALTH BENEFITS 42

CHAPTER 6. CREATING A HEALTHY PLANT-BASED EATING HABIT 51
- Build a Support Network 52

CHAPTER 7. PLANT-BASED MEAL PLAN FOR WEIGHT LOSS 53

CHAPTER 8. BREAKFAST TO MOTIVATE AND ENERGIZE YOUR BODY 56
- Why is it Important? 56

CHAPTER 9. FOOD TO EAT AND AVOID 62
- Foods to Eat 63
- Foods to Avoid 65

CHAPTER 10. BREAKFAST RECIPES 66
- Amazing Almond & Banana Granola 66
- Perfect Polenta with a Dose of Cranberries & Pears 67
- Tempeh Bacon Smoked to Perfection 68
- Delicious Quiche made with Cauliflower & Chickpea 69
- Tasty Oatmeal and Carrot Cake 71
- Onion & Mushroom Tart with a Nice Brown Rice Crust 72
- Tasty Oatmeal Muffins 74

Omelet with Chickpea Flour 75

A Toast to Remember 76

Tasty Panini 78

Amazing Blueberry Smoothie 79

CHAPTER 11.   LUNCH RECIPES 80

Stuffed Sweet Potatoes 80

Vegan Mac and Cheese 81

Satay Tempeh with Cauliflower Rice 83

Sweet Potato Quesadillas 84

Spicy Grilled Tofu with Szechuan Vegetables 86

Vegan-Friendly Fajitas 87

Incredibly Tasty Pizza 89

Rich Beans Soup 90

Delicious Baked Beans 91

Indian Lentils 92

Delicious Butternut Squash Soup 94

CHAPTER 12.   DINNER RECIPES 95

Black Bean and Veggie Soup 95

Vegetable and Tofu Skewers 97

Vegan Alfredo Fettuccine Pasta 99

Spinach Pasta in Pesto Sauce 100

No Meat Sloppy Joes 102

Acorn Squash Stuffed with Veggies and Wild Rice 103

Tofu Turkey and Drumsticks 106

CHAPTER 13.   SNACKS AND SALAD RECIPES 109

Energy Bars 109

Vegan Muffins 110

Cacao Walnut Balls 112

Almond Oats Energy Balls 112

Spicy Chickpeas 113

Peanut Butter Cups 114

Coleslaw Pasta Salad 115

Corn Avocado Salad 116

Couscous with Chickpeas Salad 117

Black & White Bean Salad 118

Quinoa with Apple & Kale 120

CHAPTER 14. SMOOTHIES RECIPES 121

Greens and Chocolate Protein Shake 121
Chocolate Black Bean Smoothie 121
Peanut Butter Protein Smoothie 122
Peanut Butter, Jelly and Date Smoothie 123
Berry and Oatmeal Smoothie 124
Vanilla Clementine Protein Smoothie 125

CHAPTER 15. DON'T FORGET TO EXERCISE 126

Tips to Keep Motivated 128
The Benefits of Exercising 130

CONCLUSION 134

PLANT-BASED HIGH-PROTEIN COOKBOOK

INTRODUCTION 140

CHAPTER 1. THE BASIC OF PLANT-BASED DIET 144

CHAPTER 2. WHAT VEGAN IS ALL ABOUT 145

CHAPTER 3. PRINCIPLES OF BODYBUILDING DIET 147

CHAPTER 4. MUSCLE GAINS & VEGANISM 153

Potential Benefits of the Vegan Bodybuilding Diet 153

CHAPTER 5. PLANT BASED DIET FOR HEALTH 156

CHAPTER 6. HIGH PROTEIN DAILY RECIPES 158

Stuffed Avocados 158
Stuffed Sweet Potatoes 159
Cauliflower with Peas 161
Burgers with Mushroom Sauce 163
Rice & Lentil Loaf 166
Chickpeas with Swiss Chard 168
Spicy Black Beans 170
Mixed Bean Soup 171
Barley & Lentil Stew 173

CHAPTER 7. BREAKFAST AND SMOOTHIE RECIPES 176

- Carrots and Raisins Muffin 176
- Easy Vegan Tacos 177
- Porridge with Oatmeal and Maca Powder 178
- Savory Potato-Turmeric Pancakes 179
- Sheer Vegan Meatza 180
- Sour Edamame Spread 182
- Stamina Tofu "Omelette" 182
- Superelan Vegan Quark Smoothie 183
- Sweet Potato and Orange Breakfast Bread 184
- The Power of Banana & Soya Smoothie 186
- Vegan Parsley and Almond Bread 187
- Vegan Sloppy Joe with Tofu 188
- Vegan Super Green Giant Smoothie 189
- Vegan Sweet "French Toast" 190
- Spinach and Blueberry Protein Drink 191
- Pick Me Up Coffee Smoothie 192
- Strawberry Vegan Smoothie 193

CHAPTER 8. LUNCH RECIPES 198

- Amazing Potato Dish 198
- Textured Sweet Potatoes and Lentils Delight 199
- Incredibly Tasty Pizza 200
- Rich Beans Soup 202
- Delicious Baked Beans 203
- Indian Lentils 205
- Delicious Butternut Squash Soup 206
- Amazing Mushroom Stew 208
- Simple Tofu Dish 209
- Special Jambalaya 210
- Delicious Chard Soup 212
- Chinese Tofu and Veggies 213
- Wonderful Corn Chowder 215
- Black Eyed Peas Stew 216
- White Bean Cassoulet 218
- Light Jackfruit Dish 220
- Veggie Curry 221

CHAPTER 9.   BURGER AND SANDWICHES 223

- Spicy Chickpea Sandwich 223
- Baked Spicy Tofu Sandwich 224
- Lentil Burgers 227
- Sweet Hawaiian Burger 228
- Tofu & Veggie Burgers 230
- Buckwheat Burgers 232

CHAPTER 10.   DINNER RECIPES 235

- Green Curry Tofu 235
- African Peanut Protein Stew 237
- Thai Zucchini Noodle Salad 239
- Split Pea and Cauliflower Stew 240
- Black Bean and Pumpkin Chili 242
- Matcha Tofu Soup 244
- Sweet Potato Tomato Soup 246
- Baked Spicy Tofu Sandwich 247
- Vegetable Stir-Fry 250
- Creamy Tomato Lentil Soup 252
- Chili Carne 254
- Mexican Lentil Stew 256
- Lentil Meatloaf 258
- Black Bean Soup 260
- Mushroom Pasta 262
- Lemon Pasta Alfredo 263

CHAPTER 11.   DESSERT AND SNACKS 266

- Banana-Nut Bread Bars 266
- Lemon Coconut Cilantro Rolls 267
- Tamari Almonds 268
- Tempeh Taco Bites 269
- Mushroom Croustades 271
- Stuffed Cherry Tomatoes 272
- Spicy Black Bean Dip 273
- French Onion Pastry Puffs 274
- Cheezy Cashew–Roasted Red Pepper Toasts 275
- Baked Potato Chips 276
- Mushrooms Stuffed With Spinach And Walnuts 278

Salsa Fresca 279

Veggie Hummus Pinwheels 281

Asian Lettuce Rolls 282

Pinto-Pecan Fireballs 283

CHAPTER 12. PRE-WORKOUT RECIPES 285

Vegan Chili 285

Sweet Potato Meal Bowls 287

Marinated Mushroom Bowls with Wild Rice and Lentils 289

Chirashi Grain Bowl 291

Mushroom Spinach Tofu Wraps 292

Mushroom Pecan Burgers 293

Healthy Vegan Tempeh 295

Broccoli Pesto with Pasta and Cherry Tomatoes 298

Mongolian Meatless Beef 299

Mexican Lentil Soup 302

CHAPTER 13. POST-WORKOUT RECIPES 304

Farro Protein Bowl 304

Teriyaki Tofu with Quinoa 305

Buddha Bowl 307

Chinese Tofu and Broccoli 309

Peanut Butter Tempeh with Rice 311

Soy Beans and Puy lentil Salad 313

Tofu and Greens Stir-Fry with Cashews 314

Spiced Crusted Tofu with Salad 315

Sprouts with Green Beans and Nuts 317

Tofu with Noodles 318

Black Bean and Seitan Stir-Fry 319

CONCLUSION 322

Plant-Based Cookbook for Athletes

The Best Plant-Based Cookbook For Athletes To Improve Heal, Increase Endurance and Strength With High-Protein Recipes

By

Joshua King

Introduction

Prioritizing a plant-based diet is not only a sustainable and more ethical choice for the environment, but it also provides the human body with a range of antioxidants, nutrients and fiber that can aid in healthy immune function, improve digestion, and enhance alertness and energy levels. Incorporating whole foods that are raw, unrefined, and unprocessed will provide the greatest benefit and absorption into the body without any immune side effects. Many animal products contain additives, stabilizers, preservatives and additional hormones that speed up the natural growth cycle of animal offspring in order to yield more meat product on the market. Not only are most animals treated inhumanely before slaughter, but they are also fed genetically modified grains and feed which are also absorbed into the human body when we consume these animals. The environmental impact of meat processing in factories and overpacked farm assemblies is also very detrimental, increasing greenhouse gas emissions, polluting the water with animal waste, releasing ammonia emissions, and clearing out natural rainforests and habitats endangering many species of plants and animals. Supporting organic and sustainable plant agriculture within our own local region has been on the rise for the last few decades and allows us to focus on the seasonal offerings of crop based on the climate of where we reside. Best of all, we can also plant seeds in our own backyard or balcony garden to reduce waste, overproduction, and eliminate our consumption of toxins and pesticides. It is also a creative and nurturing project to care for and harvest your own crop across the seasons.

Plant-based foods also include a higher amount of fiber that keeps the body feeling fuller for longer, in addition to vitamins and minerals, that many animal-based products lack in. There are many prebiotic fibers in plant-based foods such as artichokes, garlic, and onions that provide a healthy gut flora, allowing regular digestion, appetite regulation, and decreased blood sugar levels. They also help to fight inflammation which arises when the body breaks down tissues during your post-workout recovery. Green, leafy vegetables such as wheatgrass, spinach, kale, and chard can balance your blood pH levels, providing an alkalinizing effect and contain high amounts of calcium and magnesium as well. These minerals are important in enhancing bone health and density and creating greater relaxation in the body which provides better sleep at night. Plant-based foods also enhance your auto-immune system with antibodies in the long-term and provide more oxygen to the tissues, which help to fight free radicals and prevent the outgrowth of cancer and tumorous cells. Minerals such as iron, zinc, and selenium, found in high quantities in meat products are also apparent in plant-based foods such as whole grains, maple syrup, Brazil nuts, lentils, corn, garbanzo beans, bran flakes and green, leafy vegetables.

Other health benefits of consuming a plant-based diet include long-term weight loss and weight management. Overall, you will consume fewer calories but feel fuller for longer by eating foods high in fiber and protein. Plant-based proteins also take less energy and time to be broken down, allowing smoother digestion and metabolism into energy. While animal products, especially those that are heavily processed may contain trans fat which can lead to bad cholesterol, plant-based products will not create bad cholesterol unless you are overconsuming those with saturated fats such as coconut oil or corn oil.

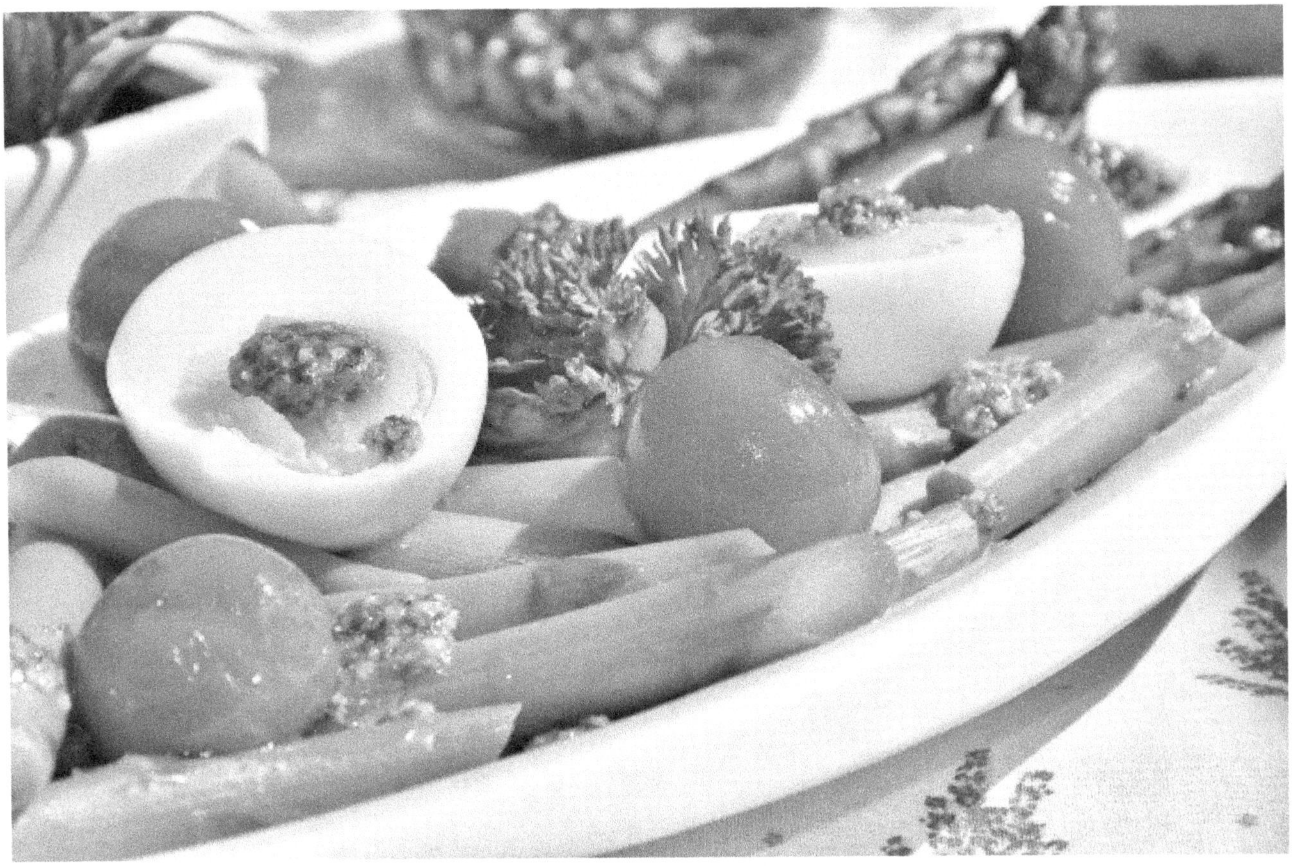

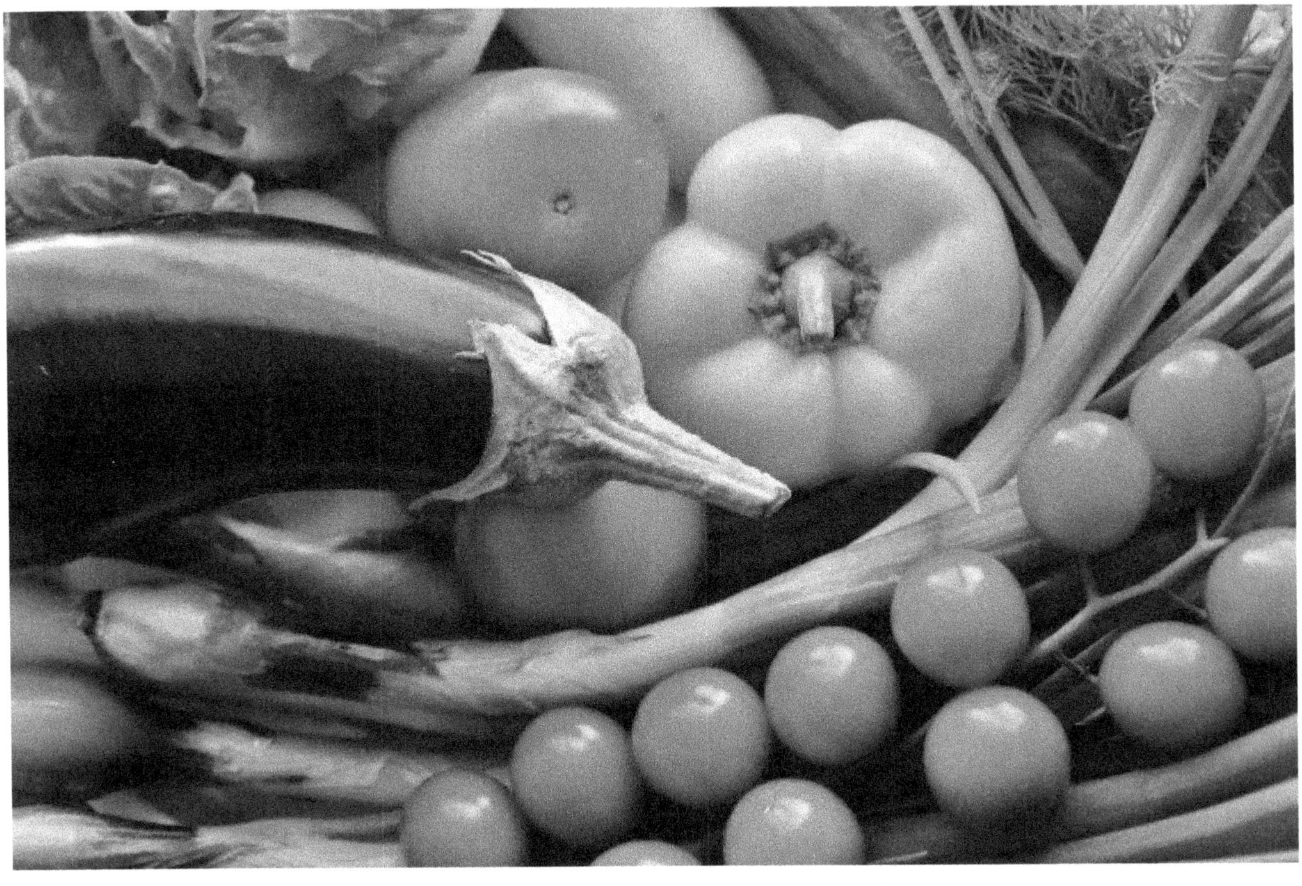

Chapter 1. What Is A Plant- Based Diet?

A plant-based diet is not synonymous to a vegetarian or vegan diet. Although these terms are often used interchangeably, they are not the same.

A plant-based diet is focused on proportionately eating more foods primarily from plants and cutting back on animal-derived foods. However, it does not necessarily involve eliminating entire food groups and lean sources of protein. This means, those on a plant-based diet may still opt to eat some meat.

Going vegan, on the other hand, means being strictly against animal products in any form—from never eating meat and dairy products to not patronizing products tested on animals and not wearing animal products such as leather.

A healthy plant-based diet generally emphasizes meeting your nutritional needs by eating more whole plant foods, while reducing the intake of animal products. Whole foods refer to natural, unrefined or minimally refined foods. Plant foods consist of those that do not have animal ingredients such as meat, eggs, honey, milk and other dairy products.

In contrast, those on a vegetarian diet may still eat processed and refined foods. Vegetarians can even eat fast foods, junk food and other salty snacks guilt-free.

Once you get started with this diet, you will notice a huge difference in how you feel each day. From the time that you wake up in the morning, you will feel that you have more energy, and that you do not get tired as easily as before. You will also have more mental focus and fewer mood-related problems.

As for digestion, a plant-based diet is also said to improve how the digestive system works. In fact, dieters confirm fewer incidences of stomach pains, bloating, indigestion and hyperacidity.

Then there's the weight loss benefit that we cannot forget about. Since a plant-based diet means eating fruits, vegetables, and whole grains that have fewer calories and are lower in fat, you will enjoy weight loss benefits that some other fad diets are not able to provide.

Aside from helping you lose weight; it maintains ideal weight longer because this diet is easier to sustain and does not require elimination of certain food groups.

Don't worry about not getting enough nutrients from your food intake. This diet provides all the necessary nutrients including proteins, vitamins, minerals, carbohydrates, fats, and antioxidants. And again, that's because it does not eliminate any food group but only encourages you to focus more on plant-based food products.

History of the Plant-based Diet

As you can imagine, humans have been consuming a plant-based diet before the invention of McDonald's and some of our other favorite fast-food chains. To begin our journey, I am going to start us off in the times of the hunter-gatherer. While we could go back even further (think Ancient Egypt!), I believe this is where a plant-based diet becomes most relevant.

Hunting and Gathering

The hunter-gatherer time period is where we find the earliest evidence of hunting. While we do have a long history of eating meat, this was a point in time where consuming meat was very limited. Of course, humans eating meat does not mean we were carnivores; in fact, the way we are built tells us differently. Yes, we can consume meat, but humans are considered omnivores. You can tell this from our jaw design, running speeds, alimentary tract, and the fact we don't have claws attached to our fingers. History also tells us we are omnivores by nature; however, the evolution of our human brains led us to become hunters so that we could survive.

The need for hunting did not come around until our ancestors left tropical regions. Other locations influenced the availability of plant-based foods. Instead of enduring winter with limited amounts of food, we had to adapt! Of course, out of hunger, animal-flesh becomes much more appealing. This early in time, our ancestors did not have a grocery store to just pop in and buy whatever they needed. Instead, they used the opportunity of hunting and gathering to keep themselves alive.

Agriculture

Eventually, we moved away from hunting and gathering and started to become farmers! While this timeline is a bit tricky and agricultural history began at different points in different parts of the world, all that matters is that at some point; animals started to become domesticated and dairy, eggs, and meat all became readily available. Once this started, humans no longer needed to hunt nor gather because the farmers provided everything we could desire!

Chapter 2. What Are The Benefits Of A Plant-Based Diet?

There are plenty of benefits associated with adopting a plant-based diet. Some people experience the positive effects of veganism earlier in the process, while others notice the advantages over a longer time frame. The benefits are common and unfold as your body becomes accustomed to the dietary changes.

- Weight loss is one of the major advantages of eating more vegetables and plant-based foods because they contain high amounts of fiber, which increases your metabolic function. Studies indicate that vegans have a lower body mass index and generally tend to be slimmer. This is largely due to the high level of fiber in vegetables and fruits, which make up a major part of the diet. Fiber helps your body process and absorb nutrients more quickly and efficiently than omnivorous or meat-based diets.

- A plant-based diet reduces your risk of cardiovascular disease. If heart conditions run in your family as an increased genetic risk, you can reduce the likelihood of a heart attack or artery damage by eating lots of fresh fruits and vegetables. Meats, and more specifically red meats such as pork and beef, contribute to the buildup of plaque in the arteries, which impacts the function of the heart. Over time, this narrows the arteries and reduces blood flow, which increases blood pressure and the risk of a heart attack.

- Vegan foods reduce inflammation caused by animal-based foods, which are highly acidic. Chronic conditions such as arthritis can cause the body to swell from inflammation, which can result in pain in specific areas of the body, and this can spread and worsen over time. While inflammation is the body's response to fighting infection and disease, it can occur incorrectly and over long time periods, thus causing constant pain. When it becomes chronic, pain management is often prescribed in the form of medication and modifications to the diet. Plant-based foods provide relief by reducing and even preventing or stopping inflammation completely once veganism becomes a regular part of your diet.

- There is a reduced risk of developing type 2 diabetes when switching from an animal-based or lacto-ovo vegetarian diet. In fact, some research indicates that the risk of developing diabetes is reduced by half. If you've already been diagnosed with diabetes, adopting a vegan diet is a much better option to manage your sugar levels. This is because the all-natural sources of sugar in fruits and vegetables are unprocessed and not excessive. When eating an animal-based diet, there is less attention to natural food sources in many cases, as vegetables and other foods take a second or third level of importance in many meals which place meat as the featured item. When you switch to plant-based eating, the quality of your food becomes more important because it's absorbed quickly, as the body digests it more efficiently than animal-based foods.

- Studies have shown a decreased risk of cancer in people who follow a plant-based diet and avoid animal and dairy products. This research indicates a link between eating red meat and cancer, due to the amount of trans fats and carcinogens these meats often contain. One of the most specific cancers that are prevented by eating a vegan diet is colon cancer. Carcinogens contribute to the accumulation of abnormal cell growth, forming cancer. In fact, proteins found in meat can increase the growth of cancerous cells and speed up the process, while vegan or vegetable-based proteins do not have the same effect.

- Eating vegan foods is better for digestion and promotes regularity while preventing constipation. This is also a great way to increase your metabolic rate and works well with a regular exercise routine. It's virtually impossible to become obese or significantly overweight while following a plant-based diet.

- You'll generally feel better and any bloating or gastric issues, including cramps, will usually disappear. A vegan diet is excellent for women of all ages and can alleviate the symptoms of menstrual cramps and discomfort as well as the side effects associated with entering menopause. A plant-based diet has all the ingredients needed to improve your way of life, including your mental, physical, and psychological well being.

Aside from the general benefits of a vegan diet, there are plenty of reasons why more athletes are going plant-based. It's become a much easier way to live and eat, with all the new meat and dairy alternatives and overall popularity. These reasons are research-based and the effects, when experienced, provide many advantages for an active lifestyle.

The benefits of a vegan diet are plentiful for bodybuilders, marathon participants, and all other types of athletes. Contrary to the myths and misconceptions about plant-based eating, there are many sources of protein, calcium, vitamins, and other nutrients to support the healthy development of muscle and tissue growth at a cellular level. A vegan diet is primarily based on natural, whole foods, leaving little or no room for processed products. It's also simpler to prepare and plan vegan meals while enjoying the advantages of creating new, delicious recipes and finding a wide range of options beyond dairy and meat.

What are the specific benefits of ditching animal products for plant-based eating? First and foremost, if you live and thrive in a physically active lifestyle, you'll need to increase your caloric intake. As an athlete, your BMI or bodyweight will be within a healthy range, and cutting calories is not recommended. At the same time, it's important not to consume an excessive number of calories, which is where a vegan diet provides some essential balance. By sticking with plant-based foods, you'll get all the nutrients and get the right amount of calories you need to maintain and improve your body and athletic performance.

An athletic lifestyle is a healthy way to live, though your risk of heart disease can remain the same if you continue eating an animal-based diet. In fact, bodybuilding and other strength training exercises can increase your heart's size and require it to function more and harder, which can be dangerous, especially if you eat a high amount of red meat and trans fats found in processed foods. A plant-based diet reduces this risk by close to 40 percent, which is significant and can help you avoid the potential for cardiac arrest in the future. You'll also have healthier arteries, blood flow, and nutrient absorption, which is due to your blood becoming more viscous or thick. When this occurs, your blood is able to transport nutrients more effectively throughout the body. This also keeps your cholesterol levels in check by preventing them from getting too high, which can contribute to many other health issues. As nutrients are better transported within the body, you will have a greater supply of oxygen which feeds the muscles and improves performance.

With a diet high in fresh fruits and vegetables, people who eat vegan will consume more antioxidants than their meat-based diet counterparts. For this reason, they are better equipped to fight and prevent diseases caused by the production of free radicals in the body. Free radicals are produced when processed, toxic foods are consumed. They can harm and interfere with the body's natural functions by encouraging the growth of tumors, cancerous cells, and various infections. Antioxidants, on the other hand, fight against and prevent the development of free radicals, protecting the body from them. When you increase the amount of these nutrients in your diet, you'll enjoy a greatly reduced risk of developing these conditions. Berries, citrus fruits, dark leafy greens, and pomegranates are great sources of antioxidants. Chia seeds are another excellent source and can be added to smoothies and plant-based desserts easily.

As you become familiar with all the options within a plant-based diet, along with these and other benefits, you'll find there are many useful options for vegan foods, including unlimited recipes and ideas, all of which are delicious and easy to prepare.

How to Prepare Before You Start a Vegan Diet

Before you dive into the world of plant-based eating, here are some important steps and suggestions to keep you focused and successful once you begin:

It's important to adapt to a plant-based diet on your own terms and at your own pace. Not everyone can ditch all animal products in one day and switch completely to vegan without making changes in stages over several weeks, even months. Every individual is different, and once you discover what works best for you, you'll be able to make those changes within your own time frame. For example, you may start by cutting down on meat or starting with dairy first. Cut out the animal foods that you don't eat as often, or eliminate one specific item at a time such as beef, chicken, or certain milk products.

Swap meat and dairy-based foods for a close vegan alternative. For example, if you normally enjoy a ham sandwich or tuna salad wrap, you may want to try hummus and smoked tempeh or tofu with sprouts as a tasty way to move into your vegan options. There are also vegan cheese slices that have similar flavors to their dairy counterparts, which can be used in the same way on subs, wraps, and sandwiches. A grilled portobello mushroom works well in place of a meat burger, and lentil stew instead of beef soup. Hummus and eggplant dips and spreads work as excellent replacements for mayonnaise and cheese options.

Don't be afraid to try new foods, including fruits and vegetables you may usually choose on your regular grocery trips. Shop at local food markets and stores specializing in imported goods. Try at least one new fruit or vegetable every two weeks, including something you might not usually eat. For some people, this might be eggplant, squash, or kale. Some of these options may not seem as favorable until you use them in a recipe. You'll discover a new exciting way to use plant-based foods. Squash, for example, may seem unappetizing to some because they haven't experienced the mellow aroma of butternut squash soup or as a roasted vegetable. If you don't feel initially comfortable trying a new food on your own, find a restaurant with the specific item in a dish. Buffets or vegan eateries are a good start and can offer many new ideas and flavors to try, inspiring and expanding your palate.

Get familiar with all the plant-based foods that provide essential nutrients, and make them a part of your regular shopping list. Beans, grains, greens, apples, berries, avocados, soy food, and other vegan options are a great foundation to build from. Consider your proteins, minerals (iron, copper, magnesium, etc.), vitamins, fiber, and other nutrients by organizing them into a chart or categories and listing foods that contain a significant source of each, as follows:

Protein - beans, soy (tofu, tempeh, miso),

Potassium - bananas, watermelon, potatoes

Vitamin C - oranges, lemon, lime, grapefruit, peppers, apples

Vitamin B/beta carotene - carrots, squash, yams/sweet potatoes

Antioxidants - berries, chia seeds

Healthy fats - avocado, flax seeds, hemp seeds, coconut oil, MCT oil

Iron - leafy greens, cabbage, beetroot

Do you have allergies or food sensitivities? Many people discover these early in life, and sometimes, intolerance for certain foods develop later in life. Peanuts, seafood, shellfish, and gluten items are common foods that certain people become allergic to or must avoid, either due to mild reactions or fatal consequences in some rare circumstances. Take note of any sensitivities you have and notice whether or not they are vegan. Many intolerances are dairy-related because some people experience difficulty with digesting lactose, which is a sugar contained in milk. Fortunately, you won't need to worry about animal-based foods that cause reactions. Going vegan most likely means reducing the number of foods you must avoid while allowing you to try new options.

Think about the plant-based foods you currently enjoy and make them a part of your diet right away. This includes meals you eat at restaurants, buffet options, and snacks you may enjoy on the go when you're commuting to work or school. Hot cereal, granola, bananas, hummus and crackers, guacamole, and vegetable side dishes are examples of what you may enjoy already and may continue to include in your diet when you completely switch to vegan foods.

Try adapting some of your favorite meat or dairy-based foods into vegan versions, such as a vegetable pasta sauce instead of meat sauce, or curried tofu instead of chicken. You may find referencing a recipe and substituting specific items with vegan options works best, or if you are a more experienced cook, try your own creations based on the dishes that inspire you.

Some people are comfortable with lacto ovo vegetarianism, which can be a step towards veganism. The lacto ovo method of eating includes dairy and eggs, without meat. For other people, a pescatarian diet works well by allowing them to eat fish while cutting out all other meats. Both of these forms of semi-vegetarianism are paths towards a fully plant-based diet.

Take time out of your schedule to explore vegan menu items, new vegan restaurants (these are usually more common than you'd think, especially in urban areas), and grocery items. While some vegan versions of cheese, dairy, and meat may seem unappealing at first, you may be pleasantly surprised by the variety of options that are available. The days of unappetizing, bland vegan substitutes are far gone, and a variety of flavorful, spicy, and aromatic blends of vegan cheese (soy or vegetable-based), coconut-cultured yogurts, nut-based and soy milk options awaits. Soy-based meat substitutes have greatly improved to the point of being indistinguishable from actual meat products, such as hamburgers and hot dogs.

Beans, legumes, and grains are an excellent and nutritious way to enhance your meals and build a foundation for them. Rice is one of the most versatile foods and can provide much-needed energy in the form of carbohydrates before a major tournament or marathon. Lentils, kidney beans, black beans, and chickpeas are all great sources of both protein and fiber. Use as many options as possible, including quinoa, couscous, oats, barley, and many other grains, as they will boost the nutrient and energy value of every meal. Explore veganism in your own way, and take your time so that you become familiar and comfortable with the switch from meat-based to plant-based. (Cook Creatively, 2016)

Ways to Boost the Benefits of a Vegan Diet

To maximize the benefits of a plant-based diet, there are some practices to keep in mind. These actions can increase the benefits of what vegan eating can do for your body and overall health:

- Eat raw whenever possible. Enjoying a meal with sauteed and stir-fried vegetables can be excellent, but if you can, try to increase the number of meals with raw food options, such as salads, hummus with a handful of peppers, cucumbers, carrots, and celery, or a fruit salad. Take advantage of raw produce toppings on veggie burgers or portobello mushroom patties. Enjoy an orange or apple in between meals as a snack or a pomegranate with your morning cereal.

- Add healthy fats to your diet. This includes monounsaturated and polyunsaturated fats, which help boost your cognitive function and provide many nutrients. You can find these in avocados, coconut oil, olive oil, nuts, and seeds. Incorporating a small handful of nuts and seeds or an avocado each day will ensure you get the right amount of fats you need in your diet. Flax and hemp seeds are also good options.

- To reduce sugar in your diet, use fruit as part of or all of a dessert option. For example, a raw, sliced mango with coconut cream is a tasty option, or try lightly baked apples sprinkled with cinnamon. A bowl of fresh berries in almond milk with or without cereal can be an excellent option for breakfast or a midday snack. If you're often on the go, bananas and apples are great options as well.

- Try a new food item once every week or two weeks. This might be something you've never tasted before, like a rare exotic fruit or vegetable, or a seed or nuts that are not commonly found in regular grocery stores. Make a point of visiting and shopping at foreign food markets and ask questions about trying new foods. Jackfruit, papaya, guava, and taro are examples of foods that are emerging in popularity in vegan cuisine and recipes.

- Add a handful of nuts and seeds to your diet whenever you need a quick snack. Making a habit of having a healthy source of eating available will make it easier.

Chapter 3. Vegan Vs Plant-Based Diet

It is quite common for people to mistake a vegan diet for a plant-based diet or vice versa. Well, even though both diets share similarities, they are not exactly the same. So, let's break it down really quick.

Vegan

A vegan diet is one that contains no animal-based products (dairy, meat, eggs as well as animal-derived products such as honey.) Someone who describes themselves as a vegan carries over this perspective into their everyday life. What this means is that they do not use or promote the use of clothes, shoes, accessories, shampoo, and makeups that have been made using material that comes from animals. Examples here include wool, beeswax, leather, gelatin, silk, and lanolin. The motivation for people to lead a veganism lifestyle often stems from a desire to make a stand and fight against animal mistreatment and poor ethical treatment of animals as well as to promote animal rights.

Plant Based Diet

On the other hand, this type of diet shares a similarity with veganism in the sense that it also does not promote dietary consumption of animal-based products. This includes dairy, meat, and eggs. The idea here is to make a diet out of minimally processed to unprocessed fruits, veggies, whole grains, nuts, seeds, and legumes. So, there will be NO Oreo cookies for you. Whole-food plant-based diet followers are often driven by the health benefits it brings. It is a diet that has very little to do with restricting calories or counting macros but mostly to do with preventing and reversing illnesses.

Benefits of Vegan Diet

There are several benefits to a vegan diet, especially when it comes to nutrition. You will consume a lot of nutrients and far less saturated fats. As great as this sounds, it can be challenging for someone to give up their animal-based foods because they need to find alternative sources of their protein, vitamins, minerals, iron, and non-saturated fats. If they don't plan their new diet carefully, it could potentially cause them to face certain health risks.

The people who go on a vegan diet may do so for more than just health reasons. They may be taking a stand to promote environmental protection and stopping animal cruelty.

Nutritional benefits:

- Reduced saturated fats: vegan diet has less saturated fats which improve health, especially when it comes to coronary diseases

- More energy: more carbs in a plant-based diet provide energy to the body , fiber: high fiber vegan diet leads to healthier bowel movement and help in fighting against colon cancer

- Anti-oxidants: vegetables and fruits are rich in antioxidants that protect the body from some types of cancer

- Vitamins: vitamins boost the immune system, heals wounds faster and benefit skin, eyes, brain, and heart.

Disease prevention:

- Cardiovascular disease: improve cardiovascular health and prevent heart attack and stroke

- Cholesterol: eliminating animal foods means eliminating dietary cholesterol which improves heart health

- Blood pressure: vegan diet is rich in whole foods which is beneficial in lowering high blood pressure

- Cancer: switching to a vegan diet reversed many illnesses like reducing chances of prostate cancer, colon cancer, and breast cancer

- Arthritis: plant-based diet is very promising for improving health in individuals suffering from arthritis

Physical benefits

- Body mass index (bmi): diet without meats lowers bmi which is an indicator of healthy weight loss
- Weight loss: vegan diet eliminates unhealthy foods that tend to cause weight gain
- Healthy skin: vitamins and other essential nutrients from vegetables makes skin healthy, so vegans have good healthy skin
- Longer life: vegan lives three to six years longer than people who don't follow a vegan or vegetarian lifestyle
- Body odor: eliminating meat and dairy product from diet reduce body odor, and body smells better
- Hairs and nails: individuals who follow a vegan diet have strong hairs and healthier nails
- Migraines and allergies: vegan diet is a relief from migraines and reduces allergy symptoms, runny nose, and congestion.

Chapter 4. Plant-Based Nutrition For Sport

Carbs and Fats - What they Are and How they Impact Performance

For athletes to achieve energy balance, they also require the right number of proteins, carbohydrates, and fats. Macronutrients provide fuel for energy expenditure and athletes need to consume them in adequate quantities. If not, it limits the availability of energy.

Athletic Performance and Carbohydrates

Carbohydrates are an essential nutrient in an athlete's diet; they enable the body to perform to its optimal standard during physical activity for two reasons:

Energy: The brain and body require energy to function; when carbohydrates are consumed and digested, they are broken down into glucose, which is stored in the muscles and liver and used as fuel during physical activity. According to Michael Gleeson, Ph.D., and Jeukendrup, Ph.D., several studies indicate that fueling the body with carbohydrates for 45 minutes or more can improve athletic performance and endurance.

Muscle Gain: When there is a limited supply of glucose in the body, other nutrients such as muscle protein and fat are used as energy. When the muscles get the right amount of carbohydrates, protein can effectively perform its primary job of repairing and rebuilding muscle tissue, which boosts muscle gain.

Carbohydrates assist athletes in performing at their best by replenishing muscle glycogen stores, which is not possible on a low-carbohydrate, high-protein diet.

Fats: The Difference Between Good and Bad

During an athletic performance, the body's main source of energy comes from carbohydrates; however, when low-intensity workouts and extensive periods of athletic activity are performed, the main energy source is from fats.

Fat is an essential part of our diet; however, to enjoy the health benefits of fat, you must understand the difference between good and bad fats. Fats from meat and dairy products are called saturated fats, and they increase the amount of bad cholesterol (low-density lipoprotein, LDL) in the blood. Those who consume excessive amounts of saturated fats increase their risk of heart disease or stroke, states the American Heart Association. A vegan diet contains limited amounts of saturated fats; they are found in foods such as cocoa butter, palm oil, and coconuts. Therefore, it is advised that those on a plant-based diet refrain from eating plant-based foods high in saturated fats. If you are going to consume these foods, ensure that they make up under 30 percent of the fat you eat.

Many plant-based foods contain monounsaturated fats, which assist in lowering LDL cholesterol, which reduces the risk of stroke and heart disease. Foods containing monounsaturated fats include walnuts, Brazil nuts, and almonds, olive oil, avocados, and tahini.

Despite the negative effects of saturated fats, their main benefit is that they increase serotonin levels. Serotonin is an important hormone that plays a role in mood regulation and is known to alleviate depression, improve sleep, and reduce feelings of anxiety.

Finally, good fats enhance the bodies nutrient absorbing capabilities, with the main nutrients being vitamins A, D, and E; as fat-soluble vitamins, they are not absorbed by the body without the assistance of healthy fats. Vitamins A, D, and E are responsible for maintaining healthy skin, creating hormones, and boosting the immune system.

How to Consume Healthy Fats on a Vegan Diet

There are many ways you can consume healthy fats on a vegan diet; here are some of them:

Cook mushrooms, winter squash, and carrots in olive oil.

Eat nuts high in unsaturated fats such as almonds after a workout. Unsaturated fats are capable of reducing inflammation; therefore, you are likely to experience reduced muscle soreness.

Use flaxseeds instead of flaxseed oil, they are both rich in healthy fats, but flaxseeds are also high in fiber.

Increase your polyunsaturated fat intake to reduce high cholesterol levels.

Educate yourself about the foods that are rich in healthy fats.

The Potential of Proteins - Why they're Crucial for Athletes

The right nutrition is essential for athletes to perform at their best. They use excessive amounts of energy during long, intensive workouts; the body also experiences changes such as muscle damage. For the body to recover, it requires sufficient rest and nutrition, which enables the following:

Muscle restoration and growth

Limits the chance of illness and injury

Gets the body ready for another intense workout

For the body to recover, it needs to replace lost sweat with electrolytes and fluids, protein to rebuild and repair muscle tissue, and carbohydrates to replenish glycogen. When it comes to recovery, protein is vital because athletes require a lot more than the average healthy person who does a limited amount of exercise.

Protein: How Much?

Athletes should consume protein 30-60 minutes after a workout to get the maximum glycogen stores and to enhance muscle protein synthesis. Between 30-60 minutes after a workout is a perfect time to restore energy with protein and carbs because protein accelerates the process of muscles converting carbohydrates into stored energy. However, if you are unable to refuel during this timeframe, just make sure you get some protein in with your snacks and meals throughout the day. Here are the recommended amounts of protein you should consume:

1 gram per pound: This amount of protein provides you with enough to build muscle.

0.82 grams per pound: There is a lot of speculation about whether 0.82 grams is enough protein to facilitate muscle growth; however, research suggests that it is, but it's the lowest amount you should consume.

1.5 grams: If you consistently go overboard with your cheat meals, 1.5 grams per pound of protein will be of benefit to you.

The extra protein will probably not result in increased gains; however, increasing your protein intake will do the following:

Will keep you full for longer

Eating more protein will force you to eat less junk because your food choices are restricted

The thermic effect of food (TEF) suggests protein is not 4 kcal per gram but closer to 3.2 kcal per gram

If you are concerned about your protein intake, you can get all your daily requirements through a well-balanced, plant-based diet with sufficient calories. You will find plenty of delicious recipes in this book as well as a detailed nutrition guide.

Plant-Based Besties - The Protein Sources for Maximum Impact

Lentils - Cooked lentils contain the following nutritional values per 125 grams:

Fat: 0.5 grams
Carbohydrates: 20 grams
Dietary fiber: 8 grams
Protein 9 grams

The Health Benefits of Lentils

Lentils are rich in polyphenols that protect the body against radiation, ultraviolet rays, heart disease, and cancer. They also help with weight maintenance and digestive health.

Broccoli - Raw broccoli contains the following nutritional values per 90 grams:

Fat: 0.3 grams
Carbohydrates: 6 grams
Dietary fiber: 2.4 grams
Protein: 2.6 grams

The Health Benefits of Broccoli

Broccoli contains several powerful nutrients such as vitamin K, which is essential for the blood clotting process, and vitamin C – a powerful antioxidant that protects the body against harmful free radicals.

Nutritional Yeast - Raw nutritional yeast contains the following nutritional values per 15 grams:

Fat: 0.5 grams
Carbohydrates: 5 grams
Dietary fiber: 3 grams
Protein: 8 grams

The Health Benefits of Nutritional Yeast

Nutritional yeast is high in vitamin B12, which helps to regulate the central nervous system, boosts energy, digestive system maintenance, protects the body against breast cancer, colon cancer, and stomach cancer. Nutritional yeast is good for people with diabetes because it contains no sugar and is therefore considered a low glycemic food.

Peanut Butter Powder - Raw peanut butter powder contains the following nutritional values per 13 grams:

Fat: 1.5 grams

Carbohydrates: 5 grams

Dietary fiber: 1 gram

Protein: 6 grams

The Health Benefits of Peanut Butter Powder

Peanut butter powder contains fewer calories and fat than regular peanut butter, making it beneficial for those wanting to reduce their fat and calorie intake. Peanut butter powder provides the same health benefits as peanut butter. It contains several nutrients that help to boost heart health, such as vitamin E, magnesium, polyunsaturated fatty acids, and monounsaturated fatty acids. It is a good source of magnesium, potassium, and iron, which improves blood circulation.

Hemp Seeds - Raw hemp seeds contain the following nutritional values per 28 grams:

Fat: 12 grams

Carbohydrates: 3 grams

Dietary fiber: 3 grams

Protein: 10 grams

The Health Benefits of Hemp Seeds

Hemp seeds are a powerful source of essential fatty acids, such as alpha-linolenic acid, which is an omega-3. They contain no trans fats, and they are low in unsaturated fats. Hemp seeds contain a wide range of vitamins and minerals, such as vitamin E, potassium, magnesium, and folate. They are high in omega-3 fatty acids, which improve heart health and reduce inflammation.

Quinoa - Raw quinoa contains the following nutritional values per 219 grams:

Fat: 2.4 grams

Carbohydrates: 25.7 grams

Dietary fiber: 2.8 grams

Protein: 5.7 grams

The Health Benefits of Quinoa

Quinoa contains almost double the amount of fiber than the majority of other grains. Fiber helps to reduce high blood pressure and therefore lower the risk of a heart attack. Quinoa is high in iron, which helps maintain the health of our red blood cells. Iron also boosts brain function because it helps carry oxygen to the brain. Quinoa is known to alleviate migraines because it assists in relaxing blood vessels.

Sprouted Whole Grain Bread - Raw sprouted whole grain bread contains the following nutritional values per slice (34 g):

Fat: 0.5 grams

Carbohydrates: 15 grams

Dietary fiber: 3 grams

Protein: 4 grams

The Health Benefits of Whole Grain Bread

Whole grains are packed with nutrients such as antioxidants, B vitamins, magnesium, copper, zinc, and iron. Studies have indicated that a diet rich in whole grains helps to reduce the risk of cancer, obesity, type 2 diabetes, and heart disease.

Tofu - Raw tofu contains the following nutritional values per 85 grams:

Fat: 3.5 grams

Carbohydrates: 2 grams

Dietary fiber: 1 gram

Protein: 8 grams

The Health Benefits of Tofu

Tofu is an excellent source of amino acids, calcium, iron, protein, and other micronutrients. Tofu comes from soy protein, which helps lower bad cholesterol. It is low in calories and gluten-free. It also contains isoflavones that protect the body against osteoporosis, heart disease, and cancer.

Chia Seeds - Dried chia seeds contain the following nutritional values for 28 grams:

Fat: 8.4 grams

Carbohydrates: 13 grams

Dietary fiber: 11 grams

Protein: 6 grams

The Health Benefits of Chia Seeds

Chia seeds are high in protein. One of the many benefits of protein is that it helps to control appetite, and therefore, plays a role in the weight loss process. Chia seeds are also rich in omega-3 fatty acids; the combination of omega-3's and protein stabilize blood sugar and improves metabolic health.

Edamame Beans - Raw edamame beans contain the following nutritional values per half a cup (75 g):

Fat: 5 grams

Carbohydrates: 9 grams

Dietary fiber: 8 grams Protein: 12 grams

The Health Benefits of Edamame Beans

Edamame beans are high in protein and low in fat, and studies indicate that people who follow a high protein, low-fat diet achieve significant weight loss because they experience less hunger between meals.

Tempeh - Raw tempeh contains the following nutritional values per 84 grams:

Fat: 6 grams

Carbohydrates: 8 grams

Dietary fiber: 5 grams

Protein: 16 grams

The Health Benefits of Tempeh

Tempeh is a highly nutritious soy product that is high in protein, prebiotics, and a wide range of vitamins and minerals. Tempeh contains calcium, but it is dairy-free;

since tempeh comes from soybeans, it contains isoflavones, which is a natural plant compound that helps reduce cholesterol levels.

Chickpeas - Raw chickpeas contains the following nutritional values per 82 grams:

Fat: 2 grams

Carbohydrates: 22 grams

Dietary fiber: 6 grams

Protein: 7 grams

The Health Benefits of Chickpeas

Chickpeas are low in calories and high in protein, which accelerates the weight loss process. They are also high in fiber, and the combination of protein and fiber assist in weight management because they suppress the appetite. Chickpeas are also considered a low glycemic food which is beneficial for blood sugar management.

Peanuts - Raw peanuts contain the following nutritional values per 32 grams:

Fat: 16 grams

Carbohydrates: 6 grams

Dietary fiber: 2 grams

Protein: 7 grams

The Health Benefits of Peanuts

Peanuts are low in carbohydrates and rich in nutrients; they contain polyunsaturated fats and monounsaturated fats. They help to improve blood cholesterol levels, which reduce the risk of stroke and heart disease. Peanuts are full of fiber and protein and help with weight maintenance. The bonus is that they also make a satisfying snack.

Almonds - Raw almonds contain the following nutritional values per 95 grams:

Fat: 47 grams

Carbohydrates: 21 grams

Dietary fiber: 12 grams

Protein: 20 grams

The Health Benefits of Almonds

Almonds are very nutritious and high in vitamins, minerals, antioxidants, and healthy fats. Almonds are rich in vitamin E, a fat-soluble antioxidant that protects the cells from oxidative stress. Several studies have linked vitamin E with lower rates of Alzheimer's disease, cancer, and heart disease.

Spirulina - Raw spirulina contains the following nutritional values per 10 grams:

Fat: 0.8 grams

Carbohydrates: 2.5 grams

Dietary fiber: 0.4 grams

Protein: 6 grams

The Health Benefits of Spirulina

Spirulina contains powerful antioxidants that protect the body against inflammation, cancer, and oxidative damage. It has a positive impact on cholesterol by lowering triglycerides and bad cholesterol at the same time as raising good cholesterol. Spirulina assists in lowering blood pressure, which helps to reduce the risk of conditions such as stroke and heart disease.

Spelt - Raw spelt contains the following nutritional values per 100 grams:

Fat: 2.4 grams

Carbohydrates: 70 grams

Dietary fiber: 11 grams Protein: 15 grams

The Health Benefits of Spelt

Spelt is rich in many nutrients such as niacin, zinc, potassium, magnesium, and iron. It is known to help reduce the cholesterol absorbed into the bloodstream. Additionally, the high fiber content in spelt helps reduce blood pressure. They lower the risk of stroke and heart disease.

Potatoes - Raw potatoes contain the following nutritional values per 1 potato (148 grams):

Fat: 0 grams

Carbohydrates: 26 grams

Dietary fiber: 2 grams

Protein: 3 grams

The Health Benefits of Potatoes

Potatoes are high in compounds such as phenolic acids, carotenoids, and flavonoids. They play the same role as antioxidants and protect the body against free radicals, thereby reducing the risk of chronic conditions such as cancer, diabetes, and heart disease. The resistant starch in potatoes also helps to improve digestive health.

Kale - Raw kale contains the following nutritional values per cup:

Fat: 0.1 grams

Carbohydrates: 1.4 grams

Dietary fiber: 0.6 grams

Protein: 0.7 grams

The Health Benefits of Kale

Kale is one of the most nutritious plants in the world, and it contains 4.5 times more vitamin C than spinach. Vitamin C is an important water-soluble antioxidant required for essential cell functions. Kale is also one of the world's best sources of vitamin K, which is crucial for blood clotting.

Mushrooms - Raw mushrooms contain the following nutritional values per half a cup (48 grams):

Fat: 0 grams

Carbohydrates: 2 grams

Dietary fiber: 1 gram

Protein: 1 gram

The Health Benefits of Mushrooms

Mushrooms are an excellent source of folic acid. They are said to help boost the health of babies while in the womb. They are also high in selenium, and studies suggest they protect against cognitive decline, thyroid disease, heart disease, and cancer.

Seitan: Raw seitan contain the following nutritional values per 100 grams:

Fat: 1.9 grams

Carbohydrates: 14 grams

Dietary fiber: 0.6 grams

Protein: 75 grams

The Health Benefits of Seitan

Seitan is a good source of protein, and it is low in calories; it is one of the few meat substitutes that doesn't contain soy. Seitan is high in iron, which increases energy and enhances athletic performance.

Chapter 5. The Incredible Health Benefits

While starting a plant-based diet is an excellent idea and has many wonderful benefits let's be honest, you are mostly here to benefit yourself. It is fantastic that you are deciding to put you and your health first! You deserve to be the best version of yourself, with a little bit of legwork, you will be there in no time!

To some people, a plant-based diet is just another fad diet. There are so many diets on the market right now, why is plant-based any different? Whether you are looking to lose weight, reverse disease, or just love animals.

A plant-based diet is so much more than just eating fruits and vegetables. This is a lifestyle where you are encouraged to journey to a better version of yourself. As you improve your eating habits, you will need something to do with all of your new found energy! It is time to gain control over your eating habits and figure out how food truly does affect our daily lives! Below, you will find the amazing benefits a plant-based diet has to offer you.

Lower Your Cholesterol

Let me start by asking you a question; how much do you think one egg affects your cholesterol? One egg a day could increase your dietary cholesterol from 97 to 418 mg in a single day! There was a study done on seventeen lacto-vegetarian college students. During this study, the students were asked to consume 400kcal in test foods along with one large egg for three weeks. During this time, their dietary cholesterol raised to these numbers. To put it in perspective, 200 to 239 mg/dL is considered borderline high.

The next question you should be asking yourself is what is considered a healthy amount of cholesterol? The answer is zero percent! There is no tolerable intake of trans fats, saturated fats, nor cholesterol. All of these (found in animal products) raise LDL cholesterol. Luckily, a plant-based diet can bring your cholesterol levels down drastically. By doing this, you will be lowering your risk of disease that is typically related to high cholesterol levels. The good news here is that your body makes the cholesterol you need! There is no need to "get it" from other sources.

Healthy Antioxidants

As of recently, there has been a push with products showing they are incredibly healthy due to the fact they contain antioxidants. These are fantastic as antioxidants help prevent the circulation of oxidized fats that are building up in your bloodstream. As you consume more antioxidants naturally in your plant-based diet, this can help reduce inflammation, lower your blood pressure, prevent blood clots, and decrease any artery stiffness you may have.

To put it into perspective, a plant can contain about sixty-four times more antioxidants compared to animal products such as meat.

High Fiber Intake

As you begin a plant-based diet, you will be getting more fiber in your diet naturally. You may be surprised to learn that on average, about ninety percent of Americans do not receive the proper amount of fiber! This is bad news for a majority of people as fiber has some very good benefits. Fiber has been shown to reduce the risk of stroke, obesity, heart disease, diabetes, breast cancer, and the risk of colon cancer! On top of these benefits, fiber also helps control blood sugar levels and cholesterol levels.

Asthma Benefits

According to the Centers for Disease Control and Prevention, about ten percent of children in 2009 has asthma. This means that in 2009, more children than adults had the risk of having an asthma attack. Asthma is defined as an inflammatory disease. The question is, what is causing the rise of asthma? It's all in the diet!

According to one study, both eggs and sweetened beverages have been linked to asthma. On the other hand, fruits and vegetables both appear to have a positive effect on lowering asthma in children that eat at least two servings of vegetables a day. In fact, their risk of suffering from an allergic asthma attack was lowered by fifty percent!

Reduce Risk of Breast Cancer

While it can be hard to pinpoint the development of breast cancer, it seems there are three steps to creating a healthier lifestyle to lower your risk of developing it in the first place. First, you will want to maintain a normal body weight. Luckily, this can be achieved by consuming a plant-based diet. On top of eating your fruits and vegetables, you will also want to limit your alcohol consumption. By doing this, individuals have been able to reduce their risk of developing breast cancer by sixty percent! To put this into perspective, meat eaters have a seventy-four percent higher risk of developing breast cancer compared to those who eat more vegetables. I'm not sure about you, but that just doesn't seem worth it to me!

Reduce the Development of Kidney Stones

Did you know that by eating one extra can of tuna a day can increase your risk of forming a calcium stone in your urinary tract by a whopping two-hundred and fifty percent? The risk is calculated by studying the relative probability of forming a stone when high animal protein is ingested. The theory behind this is that urine needs to be more alkaline if you want to lower your risk of developing stones. When meat is consumed, this produced acid in the body. On the other hand, beans and vegetables both reduce the acid in the body, leading to a lower risk of developing kidney stones; science!

Reverse and Prevent High Blood Pressure and Heart Disease

Unfortunately, one in three Americans has high blood pressure. Studies have shown that as a diet becomes plant-based, this grants the ability to drop the rate of hypertension. In fact, there is about a seventy-five percent drop between an omnivore and a vegan! It appears as though a vegetarian diet sets a kind of protection against cardiometabolic risk factors, cardiovascular disease, as well as overall total mortality. When compared against a lacto-ovo-vegetarian diet, plant-based diets seem to also have protection against cardiovascular mortality, type-2 diabetes, hypertension, as well as obesity! This is fantastic news, especially when you lean that just three portions of whole-grain foods seem to significantly reduce the risk of cardiovascular disease in middle-aged people. This is the same benefit that a symptom-reducing drug can give you!

Control and Prevent Cancer

Fat from animals is often associated with the risk of developing pancreatic cancer. In fact, for every fifty grams of chicken consumed on a daily basis, your risk of developing pancreatic cancer increases by seventy-two percent! At this point in time, pancreatic cancer is the fourth most common death-causing cancer in the world. It's pretty simple to avoid if you simply switch your beef to beans!

On the other end of the spectrum, it appears that by consuming 70g of more beans a day can cut your risk of developing colon cancer by seventy-five percent. This may be due to IP which is found in cereal and beans. It appears this plays a major role in controlling tumor-growth, metastasis and preventing cancer. In addition to these benefits, IP overall seems to enhance the immune system, lower elevated serum cholesterol, prevent calcification and kidney stones, as well as reducing pathological platelet activity within the body. That seems pretty nifty for eating just a few more beans and less meat!

Decrease Insulin Resistance

Our bodies are very delicate machines. When fat begins to accumulate in your muscle cells, this interferes with insulin. When this build up happens, the insulin in the body is unable to bring the sugar out of the blood system that your body needs for energy. Unfortunately, high sugar intake makes this situation even worse and can clog your arteries altogether. When you eliminate meat from the diet, this means you will have less fat in your muscles. By decreasing these levels, you will be able to avoid insulin resistance in the first place!

Reverse and Prevent Diabetes

As of right now, diabetes is the cause of 750,000 deaths each year. Since 1990, the number of individuals in the United States diagnosed with diabetes has tripled to more than twenty million people. Within this range, you have one-hundred and thirty-two thousand children below the age of eighteen years old who suffer from diabetes. In 2014, fifty-two thousand people were diagnosed with end-age renal disease due to diabetes. Overall, the United States spent a total of two hundred and forty-five billion dollars in direct cost of diagnosing individuals with diabetes. If these numbers seem overwhelming to you, I have good news; plant-based diet can help with this issue. As you learn how to incorporate more vegetables into your diet, the risk of developing hypertension and diabetes drops by about seventy-eight percent.

Obesity Control and Weight Loss

In a study completed on various diet groups, it was shown that beans typically have a lower mass index compared to other individuals. These people were also proven to be less prone to obesity when they were compared to both vegetarians and non-vegetarians. This may be due to the fact that plant-based individuals have lower animal intake and higher fiber intake. When you reduce your caloric intake to lose weight at an unhealthy level, this has the ability to lead to unhealthy coping mechanisms such as bulimia and anorexia. As you learn how to follow a plant-based diet, you will be filling up on healthy foods such as vegetables, fruits, nuts, and whole grains. At no point on this diet should you be starving or wishing you could eat more. All of the food you will be consuming are typically low in fat and will help with weight loss.

Healthier Bones

One of the common misconceptions around a plant-based diet is that due to the fact you will no longer be drinking cow's milk, you will be lacking the calcium your bones need to grow strong. While we will be going over this further in depth later, all you need to know now is that it simply is not true. While on a plant-based diet, you will be receiving plenty of essential nutrients such as vitamin K, magnesium, and potassium; all of which improve bone health.

A plant-based diet helps maintain an acid-base ratio which is very important for bone health. While on an acidic diet, this aids in the loss of calcium during urination. As you learned earlier, the more meat you consume, the more acidic your body becomes. Luckily, fruits and vegetables are high in magnesium and potassium which provides alkalinity in your diet.

Along the same lines, green leafy vegetables are filled with vitamin K that you need for your bones. Studies have shown that with an adequate amount of vitamin K in your diet, this can help reduce the risk of hip fractures. Along with these studies, research has also shown that soy products that have isoflavones also have a positive effect on bone health in women that are postmenopausal. By having a proper amount of isoflavones, this helps improve bone mineral density, reduce bone resorption, and helps improve overall bone formation. Overall, less calcium loss leads to reducing your risk of osteoporosis, even when calcium intake is low!

Do it for the Animals

Whether or not you are switching to a plant-based diet for reasons other than health, it never hurts to be kind and compassionate toward other sentient beings. At the end of the day, sparing someone's life is going to be the right thing to do, especially when they never asked to be brought into this world in the first place.

Unfortunately, this is the whole reason behind the dairy and meat industry. In all honesty, there is nothing humane about taking lives or animal farming.

Of course, this goes beyond meat products. There are also major issues with the egg and dairy industry where dairy cows are forcefully impregnated and then have their calves taken away so we can steal their milk. These animals have feelings and emotions just like we do, what gives us the right to use them for their worth and then throw them away like garbage when we no longer have a use for them? Do the animals a favor and eat more plants, it will be better on your conscious.

Along with these same lines, you never know what is going to come with your animal products. There are a host of toxins, dioxins, hormones, antibiotics, and bacteria that can cause some serious health issues. In fact, there is a very high percentage of animal flesh that is contaminated with dangerous bacteria such as E. coli, listeria, and Campylobacter. These are all tough to find some time because these bacteria live in the flesh, feces, and intestinal tracts of the animals.

With the bacteria being tough to find and kill, this eventually can cause food poisoning. Each year, the USDA has reported that animal flesh causes about seventy percent of food poisoning per year. This means that there are about seventy-five million cases of food poisoning a year, five-thousands of which result in death.

Do it for the Environment

We were given this one planet to live on, and we should be doing everything in our power to help protect it. During these trying times, it seems that half of the population believes in climate change while the other half thinks of it as fake news. As a plant-eater, it is our duty to do our part in saving the environment. Unfortunately, the meat and farming industry is going to be a hard beast to take down. Depending on the source, it has been proven that the meat industry is behind anywhere from eighteen to fifty-one percent of man-made pollution. This puts the farm industry ahead of transportation when it comes down to the contribution of pollution to the greenhouse effect. In one pound of hamburger meat that you are consuming, this equals about seventy-five kg of CO_2 emission. Do you know what produces that much CO_2 emission? Three weeks from using your car! Do your part, eat more plants and save the planet.

Improve your Mood

When you are making an impact on saving the animals and saving the environment, it is no surprise that your mood will enhance! As you begin to cut back on animal products, you will be abstaining from the stress hormones those animals are producing while they are on their way to the slaughterhouse. This factor alone will have a major impact on your mood stability. By eating plants, this helps individuals lower their levels of fatigue, hostility, anger, depression, anxiety, and overall tension. The mood boost may be due to the antioxidants mentioned earlier in this chapter.

On top of these added benefits, it seems as though carbohydrate-rich foods like rye bread, steel cut oats, and brown rice all seem to have a positive effect on the serotonin levels in the brain. Serotonin is very important in controlling mood which is why a plant-based diet may help treat the symptoms that are often associated with depression and anxiety.

Skin and Digestion Improvements

You may be surprised to learn that skin and digestion are actually connected! If you suffer from acne-prone skin, dairy may be the culprit behind the issue! If you have bad acne, try a plant-based diet. As you eat more fruits and vegetables, you will be eliminating fatty foods such as oils and animal products that may be causing the acne in the first place. On top of this, fruits and vegetables are often rich in water and can provide you with high levels of minerals and vitamins. By consuming more fiber in your diet, this helps eliminate toxins in your body and boost digestion. When this happens, it could clear up your acne!

Improve Overall Fitness

Amazing things will happen as you lose weight and clean yourself from the inside out. When people first begin a plant-based diet, there is a common misconception that a lack of animal products means a lack of muscle mass and energy. Luckily, the opposite is true. It seems as though meat and dairy are both harder to digest. When these products are harder to digest, this means that it is taking more energy to do so. As you consume more fruits and vegetables on a plant-based diet, you will be amazed at how much added energy and strength you will develop.

On top of these benefits, a plant-based diet provides you with plenty of great quality proteins if you are looking to build muscle mass. While eating legumes, nuts, seeds, green vegetables, and whole grains, you will easily be consuming the forty to fifty grams of protein per day that is recommended. Of course, this number will vary but depending on your goals; you will easily be able to consume plenty of protein on a plant-based diet.

It's So Easy

When you first begin a plant-based diet, you should just expect your friends and family to doubt your life choices. You will be amazed to learn just how easy it is to live plant-based in the modern age. At the grocery store alone, there are incredible plant-based options for you and your family. There are plenty of plant-based milk options, ice creams, mock meats and more. Now, you are no longer forced to cook at home if you wish to live this lifestyle. With each passing day, becoming a plant-based person is become much easier compared to earlier times.

Chapter 6. Creating A Healthy Plant-Based Eating Habit

A common misconception among many people – even some of those in the health and fitness industry is that anyone who switches to a plant-based diet automatically becomes super healthy. There are tons of plant-based junk foods out there which can really derail your health goals if you are constantly consuming them. Committing to healthy foods is the only way that you can achieve health benefits. On the other hand, these plant-based snacks do play a role in keeping you motivated. They should be consumed in moderation, sparingly and in small bits.

Decide What a Plant-Based Diet Means for You Making a decision to structure how your plant-based diet is going to look is the first step, and it is going to help you transition from your current diet outlook. This is something that is really personal and varies from one person to the other. While some people decide that they will not tolerate any animal products at all, some make do with tiny bits of dairy or meat occasionally. It is really up to you to decide what and how you want your plant-based diet to look like. The most important thing is that whole plant-based foods have to make a great majority of your diet.

Understand What You Are Eating All right, now that you've gotten the decision part down, your next task is going to involve a lot of analysis on your part. What do we mean by this? Well, if this is your first time trying out the plant-based diet, you may be surprised by the number of foods, especially packaged foods, which contain animal products. You will find yourself nurturing the habit of reading labels while you are shopping.

Find Revamped Versions of Your Favorite Recipes I'm sure you have a number of favorite dishes that are not necessarily plant based. For most people, leaving all that behind is usually the hardest part. However, there is still a way you could meet halfway. Take some time to ponder what you like about those non-plant-based meals. Think along the lines of flavor, texture, versatility and so on; and look for swaps in the whole food plant-based diet that can fulfill what you will be missing.

Just to give you some insight into what I mean, here are a couple of examples: Crumbled or blended tofu would make for a decent filling in both sweet and savory dishes just like ricotta cheese would in lasagna. Lentils go particularly well with saucy dishes that are typically associated with meatloaf and Bolognese.

All in all, when this is executed right, you will not even miss your non-plant based favorite meals.

Build a Support Network

Building any new habit is tough, but it doesn't have to be. Find yourself some friends, or even relatives, who are willing to lead this lifestyle with you. This will help you stay focused and motivated while also providing emotional support and some form of accountability. You can do fun stuff like trying out and sharing new recipes with these friends or even hitting up restaurants that offer a variety of plant-based options. You can even go a step further and look up local plant-based groups on social media to help you expand your knowledge and support network.

Chapter 7. Plant-Based Meal Plan For Weight Loss

Vegan athletes need to be aware of what they eat and how much they eat to absorb the required nutrition that supports muscle function, repair, endurance, strength, and motivation as these are qualities that professional athletes treasure. Protein features high on the list of what to eat (Preiato, 2019). You should also consider your calorie macro and micro nutritional sources and amino acids, some of which may need to be supplemented. Proteins and carbohydrates average at four calories per gram, while fats average at nine calories per gram. Following this, it is possible to calculate how much of each nutrient type to consume per day.

When planning your vegan diet, an athlete may need to consider their exercise routines, as those who gym may have high impact days (such as the dreaded "leg-day") and lower impact days where their bodies need more nutrients geared at repair work. For every athlete, their meal plans will be uniquely based on their age, weight, level of activity, food availability (veggies and fruits tend to be seasonal), and personal taste. You certainly don't have to eat buckets of beans to be a vegan.

Pulling It All Together Into Your Meal Plan

In planning your vegan diet, you might consider the above graph, which guides your per daily grams for the average vegan based on a 1,525 calorie diet. For athletes, the amounts will increase to accommodate the calories burned during exercise. Hence, if you burn 500 calories running for an hour, you need to increase your diet by consuming an additional 125 grams of protein or carbs.

From the above graph, it is possible to plan meals based on the daily grams per nutrient type. You might get your base line 160 grams protein as follows: 1 cup wheat gluten (75 grams), 1 cup soy beans (68 grams), and ½ cup tofu (20 grams). The 100 grams carbs could be gained from: two slices of whole wheat bread (30 grams); one fruit, like apples, bananas, oranges, or pears (45 grams total); ½ cup granola (15 grams), and ½ English muffin (15 grams). Daily fat requirements can be made up by eating 100 grams of nuts and seeds (perhaps with the granola and fruit, yum!).

The 20 grams of amino acids could be spread throughout any of the plant foods consumed in this diet or supplemented via a nutritional supplement or dietary shake. These quantities would be split into three or more meals, depending on your metabolism and workout times. Increases to the calorie amounts depend on your activities. Simply rework the grams per day based on this. (Remember the fast rule: carbs and proteins (1 gram=4 calories) and fats (1 gram=9 calories). It is better to increase your carb and protein intake (in combination) than the fat intake.

Tips for Success

Converting to the vegan diet from an omnivore diet may, surprisingly, be a huge mental shock; however, there are some changes to your digestive system to consider as well. Vegans consume more dietary fiber than most omnivores, hence, your gut may go through stages of feeling somewhat bloated. You will need to consume more water as well. There are many suggested ratios, yet the easiest is to work per calorie. A fast rule of 1 milliliter water per calorie seems easy enough to follow. Keeping in mind that the volume of your food may increase, you may also need to eat quite a while earlier than an omnivore would before exercising. So, the usual rule of an hour fast before eating may need to be extended to 90 minutes fast before exercising.

Always consider adding variety to your vegan diet as this increases the opportunity for your body to consume all of the essential amino acids, and this leads to better protein synthesis (which is essential for developing muscle tone and recovering from injuries). Plant-based meals are very filling due to their high fiber content, yet you need to consume a larger amount to meet your calorie requirements. To avoid feeling too sated, you can gain extra carbs from eating nuts and seeds throughout the day as snacks.

Finally, when adding the finishing touches to your training program, it is essential that you intersperse training sessions with sufficient time to ensure that your muscles have time to rest and recover (where you rebuild their energy reserves, hydrate your body, and restore the normal chemical balance of your metabolism). Short-term rest periods may be anything from taking a few minutes break before moving on to the next training activity or even taking the rest of the day off after a particularly strenuous session. Professional athletes know that the body may be a machine, but it is a machine that needs to have "down time" too. It may be a good idea to keep a training log where you record what you have eaten, how long you fasted before training, and how you felt during and after the training session. This will also help you to evaluate whether you need to add more carbs or proteins to your diet, and if you require a longer rest period before moving on to the next training activity.

If you struggle with fatigue (or the shakes) after strenuous activities, you may need to increase your amino acid consumption or get more zinc and iron into your system. After all, we are all unique, and what works for another vegan athlete may not work for you. This training log can also allow you to experiment with perhaps moving to shorter training sessions with more frequent rest periods to achieve the same level of fitness and muscle building. No two professional athletes train the same way. Listen to your body and your gut to find a way that works for you.

Lastly, don't forget to get enough sleep. Mental fatigue can easily translate as physical symptoms. Insomnia may also be caused by a deficiency in magnesium. This could be caused by strenuous activity that consumes natural minerals in the body. Taking a magnesium supplement or eating some dark chocolate or half a banana before sleep can help create restful sleep.

Fortunately, the Internet allows for the development of support networks for vegan athletes. What we eat says a lot about us, and vegans can be successful, high-achieving athletes with planning and experimentation to find what works for their unique body.

Chapter 8. Breakfast To Motivate And Energize Your Body

Why is it Important?

There is a saying that describes breakfast as being the most important meal of the day. Why is that? After a good night's sleep, your body needs to be replenished with healthy levels to ensure the proper function of the muscles and brain. It is also partially dehydrated. The glycogen stored in the liver through carbohydrates is depleted. Cortisol levels are higher, as well. It is a hormone responsible for breaking down muscle.

According to Tim Ziegenfuss, "skipping breakfast drop kicks your coordination, stifles concentration, and puts a straitjacket on alertness." He is the International Society for Sports Nutrition's president. Then, skipping breakfast will weaken your muscle strength and endurance.

You see, breakfast is what gets your metabolism going. It is responsible for burning calories that you ingest throughout the day. On the downside, skipping breakfast will conserve calories instead. It is wrong to think that omitting breakfast means fewer calories because you risk having a higher body mass index. BMI is the ratio used to determine a person's healthy weight range. It is calculated by comparing their weight to their height. A higher BMI suggests you might be overweight. Those who eat breakfast are generally slimmer because starting the day with protein and fiber keeps your food intake in check for the rest of the day.

Other advantages to starting your day with a nutritious meal are a higher intake of calcium and fiber, the consumption of additional fruits and vegetables, and better performance in the execution of tasks. The same applies to exercise. It gives you energy, helps you stay focused and get things done. Eating breakfast also is linked to lower cholesterol levels and reduced risk of getting a chronic disease. Additionally, it facilitates mental faculties, such as concentration and memory.

However, those who don't have breakfast are more likely to make unhealthy food choices for the rest of the day. There is also an increased risk of developing other bad habits and risky behaviors.

Athletes realize that the best investment they can make is their health. That means fitness enthusiasts should favor a satisfying meal over a few extra minutes of shut-eye. Saying you don't have enough time to eat breakfast, aren't hungry, or don't like eating breakfast foods are excuses that will affect your performance.

Therefore, dieticians suggest you eat a more copious breakfast, one with anywhere between 500-700 calories. Not only will it provide you with energy, but limit cravings and keep hunger at bay. On the other hand, if you plan on working out first thing in the morning, a half-breakfast will suffice. Doing so will prolong your workout and enhance your physical activity. Even a simple breakfast is better than eating nothing at all.

Oatmeal

What are oats? They are considered one of the healthiest grains on the planet. They are sources of whole grains and are nutrient-dense. They also have a chockfull of vitamins and minerals, antioxidants, and fiber. Some health benefits that come with incorporating oats into your diet are a reduced risk of chronic disease, weight loss, and lower levels of sugar in the blood. Oats are good sources of fiber, protein, and carbohydrates. Antioxidants found in oats lower blood pressure.

They also contain soluble fibers that reduce cholesterol, increase satiety, and promote the growth of good bacteria in your gut.

A popular way of eating oats is in oatmeal. Here is a basic recipe for making oatmeal that you can customize to include the ingredients you love.

Casseroles

If you own a slow cooker, then you know how wonderful it is. Think of how practical it is for your food to cook overnight and be ready when you wake up the next day. Breakfast casseroles can be made ahead of time. Since it is cooked in one dish, you won't have as many dishes to wash. It is quick and easy to throw together and is bursting with flavor.

In some of our plant-based recipes like this one, you will see nutritional yeast on the ingredient list. What is it? It's from the same yeast used for brewing and baking, but with added nutrients. In this guide, we recommend vegans use fortified nutritional yeast as a source of vitamin B-12 that is typically only found in meat. Vegans are more at risk of having a deficiency of this vitamin in their diet. Nutritional yeast comes in different formats, such as powder, granules, or flakes. So why is it right for you? It is a complete protein because it has all nine essential amino acids. It also has minerals that help regulate the metabolism. In addition to this, this food has antioxidants, and it can strengthen one's immunity. It helps lower bad cholesterol, too.

In this recipe, it will be used as a cheese flavoring, without the dairy. Other ways that it can be a part of your everyday cooking is as a seasoning over popcorn, in giving an umami flavor in soups or as a thickener in sauces. Just one tablespoon or two of nutritional yeast will provide you with your recommended daily amount of vitamin B12.

Muffins

These aren't your typical coffee shop muffins that you grab with a coffee to go. No, these are much healthier! Our vegan breakfast muffins are kind on the planet, too — many baking recipes animal by-products, but not when you can substitute them with a vegan egg. Simply mix one tablespoon of flaxseed meal with 2 ½ tablespoons of water.

Bran cereal is a great breakfast choice for athletes. It is jam-packed with fiber and other nutrients like zinc and copper, selenium, and manganese. Its' flavor can vary between being sweet and nutty. In recipes, it is used to add texture and taste. Bran also aids in digestion, as it helps regulate bowel movement and reduces constipation. It is rich in prebiotics, which promotes a healthy gut. Eating bran on a regular basis can reduce your risk of getting certain types of cancer and can improve cardiovascular health.

Yogurt Parfaits

What is there not to love about yogurt? It is creamy and sweet. Vegans have found a way of enjoying yogurt without dairy products. This is thanks to nuts like cashews and almonds, amongst other things.

Why is vegan yogurt good for you? Some probiotics help keep your digestive tract healthy. The nuts used to make non-dairy milk such as almonds and cashews are full of protein, fiber, and healthy fats. They also contain calcium, antioxidants, iron, magnesium, zinc, and vitamins C and E. These nutrients are beneficial for regulating blood sugar levels, decrease the wrong kind of cholesterol and help burn fat more efficiently. Regular yogurt can have ingredients like artificial coloring and flavoring, which isn't right for you. It also has dairy, which we know is a food that is responsible for animal cruelty.

To make a yogurt parfait, you simply alternate between layers of yogurt with granola and fruit. It is a feast to the eyes as much as it is nutritious. You can buy non-dairy yogurt at the grocery store. Alternatively, you can make it yourself. There are many ways to go about it, but we'll keep this sweet and simple.

Pudding

Who says that pudding is only for dessert? With the right ingredients, this snack can be turned into a filling breakfast that will kickstart your day.

Let's take a minute to talk about chia seeds. This superfood is a significant element to include in a vegan athlete's diet. They have fatty acids from Omega 3, are a good source of antioxidants and are high in iron, fiber, calcium (18% of your daily intake) and protein. In just one tablespoon of chia seeds, you have 5 grams of fiber! Chia seeds can also be mixed with water to imitate the texture and moistness of an egg.

There are several ways of eating this versatile food. When raw, it can be used as a topping in smoothies, oatmeal cereal, and yogurt. In water, the seeds will expand and get a jelly-like texture. That is because chia seeds grow in volume. It is quite impressive when you think how this small seed can absorb up to 27 times its' weight from the liquid it is soaking in.

Scrambled Eggs

Eggs are a staple item in a person's breakfast routine and are known to provide athletes with protein and other nutrients. We will show you how vegans enjoy scrambled eggs by talking about tofu. This product comes from soya. To prepare the tofu, you need to press the soy milk into a block and then cool it.

The soy milk curd is what holds it together.

ofu varies in texture and firmness. Its' origins are from China but have been embraced by European and Western countries to promote healthy eating.

Tofu provides nine essential amino acids that the body needs to function correctly. It is also a good source of protein. Other nutrients that make tofu a popular food item in a vegan diet are its' other health benefits. It is rich in vitamin B1, copper, zinc, manganese, magnesium, and phosphorus.

Why do vegan athletes love avocados?

They have numerous health benefits, as well. Some of these include healthy fats and many vitamins. Avocadoes are good sources of Vitamin B-6, C, E, and K. They also have minerals like magnesium, potassium, riboflavin, and niacin. Plant-based foods such as fruits and vegetables are known to reduce the risk of developing chronic disease. Avocadoes do this and more. They also give you more energy, manage weight, and do wonders for your complexion. Monosaturated fats help satisfy hunger and stabilize blood sugar levels. Studies are even suggesting that avocados are beneficial for strengthening your immune system.

They are suitable for your cardiovascular health, too. The green fruit has beta-carotene, as well, which supports good vision. Vitamin K in avocados promotes bone health and can aid in preventing osteoporosis. A nutrient found in avocados, folate, helps decrease depression symptoms. It is high in fiber and can facilitate digestion.

Chapter 9. Food To Eat And Avoid

Why select in food options?

Any method that contains food and diet comes with a defined range of food options that you can select and avoid. It is necessary to pick up the right kind of food that will help you to get the desired results in the end. Making the food option is necessary as you have restrictions in the use of dietary options. Every meal plan defines the use of specific food options because all the food items have a significant effect on your body. Therefore, it is necessary to make the definition of the food options you need to use or lose in the meal plan.

Meeting nutrients

The basic need of selecting the food options is nutrition. When you are cutting off the other food options from the diet chart and moving towards the herbs and plants only then you need to choose the better options. Your body needs remain the same while the intake is different then you need to meet and match all the body requirements by selecting the nutrients that can help to get better with your overall body growth and its maintenance. The plant-based diet allows you to get all the necessary options that help you to meet the nutrient value your body needs.

Getting better taste

When you are taking a specific diet plan, it is hard to get the variant taste for your taste buds. It is important for you to make sure that you will choose the multiple food options that can help you to have better taste. The food selection you will make is to help you with a better approach towards the diet plan and it will not bore you.

Make new combinations

A plant-based diet helps you to get in shape, be healthy and improve your body's immunity as well. In contrast, it can make you feel sick, as you will be using only the plant products nothing else. In this regard, you need to have an idea about the best products. These multiple and best products will help you to make new combinations for your meals and help you to progress well with your diet option too. If you are not paying attention to new combinations, then it will not be possible for you to have continued interest in this diet plan. Soon you will get bored with the plan and want to quit and that can terminate your results. It is important to be consistent and maintain your interest in the food options you have around in order to get the best results.

Foods to Eat

If you are just getting started with the vegan diet, the food restrictions may come across daunting. Essentially, you will be limiting your food choices to plant-based foods. Luckily, there is a very long list of foods that you will be able to eat while following this diet. Below are some of the foods that you can include on your diet—so you go into your vegan journey, full of knowledge!

Vegetables and Fruits

Obviously, fruits and vegetables are going to be very high on your list. At this point in your life, you are most likely familiar with preparing some of your favorite dishes in a certain way. It should be noted that on the vegan diet, all dairy products such as buttermilk, cream, yoghurt, butter, cheese, and milk are going to be eliminated. With, there are some incredible alternatives such as coconut and soy. It will take a little bit of time to adjust, but you may find that you enjoy these alternatives even more—especially because they are going to be better for your health!

There will be many vegetables you can consume on the vegan diet. It will be important for you to learn how to balance your choices so you can consume all the nutrients you need. Within this chapter, you will be provided with a list of high-protein foods—but you will also need to consume foods such as kale, broccoli, and book choy to help with calcium levels.

Seeds, Nuts, and Legumes

As noted earlier, protein is going to be important once you remove animal products from your diet. The good news is that legumes are a wonderful plant-based and low-fat product for vegans to get their protein. You will be eating plenty of beans such as peanuts, pinto beans, split peas, black beans, lentils, and even chickpeas. There are unlimited ways to consume these foods in several different dishes.

You will also be eating plenty of seeds and nuts. Both foods help provide a proper amount of protein and healthy fats when consumed in moderation. It should be noted that nuts are typically high in calories, so if you are looking to lose weight while following the vegan lifestyle, you will have to limit your portions. These foods should also be consumed without salt or sweeteners for added health benefits.

Whole Grains

Another food that will be enjoyed while following a Vegan diet is whole grains! There are several products you will be able to enjoy such as wild rice, rye, quinoa, oats, millet, barley, bulgur, and brown rice! You can include these foods in any meal whether it be breakfast, lunch, or dinner! It should be noted that you will need to change how you serve some of your favorite foods. You will have to say goodbye to any animal-based products and instead, try to include more vegetables and olive oil. You can still have your morning oatmeal, but you'll have to make the switch to almond or soymilk.

Vegan Food Products and Substitutions

On the modern market, you will see several vegan-friendly products that have been manufactured. Some of these products include vegan mayo, whipped cream, "meat" patties, and other frozen foods. While these are great to have on hand, they are still processed foods. You will want to be careful of foods that have added sugar and salts. Any excessive additives will undo the incredible benefits the vegan diet has to offer. While, of course, they are always an option, you should try your best to stick with whole foods.

Foods to Avoid

Poultry, Meat, and Seafood

Obviously, this is a given. These foods include quail, duck, goose, turkey, chicken, wild meat, organ meat, horse, veal, pork, lamb, and beef. An easy rule you can follow is that if it has a face or a mother, leave it out. You will also have to leave out any type of fish or seafood. These include lobster, crab, mussels, calamari, scallops, squid, shrimp, anchovies, and any fish.

Dairy and Eggs

Removing dairy and eggs from a diet is typically one of the hardest parts of becoming a vegan. When you are unable to put your favorite creamer into your coffee, or simply make a batch of brownies because you must use eggs, you will notice the major difference. If you wish to become vegan, you will have to find alternatives for ice cream, cream, butter, cheese, yoghurt, milk, and any type of egg.

Animal-Based Ingredients

Animal-based ingredients are where you will have to be careful. I suggest learning how to read food labels so you can watch for tricky ingredients. You will want to avoid ingredients such as shellac, isinglass, carmine, cochineal, gelatine, egg white albumen, lactose, casein, and whey. You will also be avoiding animal-derived vitamin D3 as well as fish-derived omega-3 fatty acids.

Chapter 10. Breakfast Recipes

Amazing Almond & Banana Granola

Servings: 16

Calories: 248.9

Preparation Time: 5 minutes

Cooking Time: 70 minutes

Ingredients:

2 peeled and chopped ripe bananas

8 cups of rolled oats

1 teaspoon of salt

2 cups of freshly pitted and chopped dates

1 cup of slivered and toasted almonds

1 teaspoon of almond extract

Nutrition:

Fat: 9.4 g

Carbohydrate: 35.9 g

Protein: 7.6 g

Directions:

Preheat the oven to 275o F.

Line two 13 x 18-inch baking sheets with parchment paper.

In a medium saucepan, add 1 cup of water and the dates, and bring to a boil. On medium heat, cook them for about 10 minutes. The dates will be soft and pulpy. Keep on adding water to the saucepan so that the dates do not stick to the pan.

After removing the dates from the heat, allow them to cool before you blend them with salt, almond extract, and bananas.

You will have a smooth and creamy puree.

Add this mixture to the oats, and give it a thorough mix.

Divide the mixture into equal halves and spread over the baking sheets.

Bake for about 30-40 minutes, stirring every 10 minutes or so.

You will know that the granola is ready when it becomes crispy.

After removing the baking sheets from the oven, allow them to cool. Then, add the slivered almonds.

You can store your granola in an airtight container and enjoy it whenever you are hungry.

Perfect Polenta with a Dose of Cranberries & Pears

Servings: 4

Calories: 185

Preparation Time: 5 minutes

Cooking Time: 10 minutes

Ingredients:

2 pears freshly cored, peeled, and diced

1 batch of warm basic polenta

¼ cup of brown rice syrup

1 teaspoon of ground cinnamon

1 cup of dried or fresh cranberries

Nutrition:

Fat: 4.6 g Protein: 5 g Carbohydrate: 6.1 g

Directions: Warm the polenta in a medium-sized saucepan. Then, add the cranberries, pears, and cinnamon powder. Cook everything, stirring occasionally. You will know that the dish is ready when the pears are soft. The entire dish will be done within 10 minutes. Divide the polenta equally among 4 bowls. Add some pear compote as the last finishing touch. Now you can dig into this hassle-free breakfast bowl full of goodness.

Tempeh Bacon Smoked to Perfection

Servings: 10

Calories: 130

Preparation Time: 5 minutes

Cooking Time: 40 minutes

Ingredients:

3 tablespoons of maple syrup

8-ounce packages of tempeh

¼ cup of soy or tamari sauce

2 teaspoons of liquid smoke

Nutrition:

Carbohydrate: 17 g

Protein: 12 g

Fat: 1 g

Directions:

In a steamer basket, steam the block of tempeh.

Mix the tamari, maple syrup, and liquid smoke in a medium-sized bowl.

Once the tempeh cools down, slice into stripes and add to the prepared marinade. Remember: the longer the tempeh marinates, the better the flavor will be. If possible, refrigerate overnight. If not, marinate for at least half an hour.

In a sauté pan, cook the tempeh on medium-high heat with a bit of the marinade.

Once the strips get crispy on one side, turn them over so that both sides are evenly cooked.

You can add some more marinade to cook the tempeh, but they should be properly caramelized. It will take about 5 minutes for each side to cook.

Enjoy the crispy caramelized tempeh with your favorite dip.

Delicious Quiche made with Cauliflower & Chickpea

Servings: 2-4

Calories: 156.3

Preparation Time: 10 minutes

Cooking Time: 30 minutes

Ingredients:

½ teaspoon of salt

1 cup of grated cauliflower

1 cup of chickpea flour

½ teaspoon of baking powder

½ zucchini, thinly sliced into half moons

1 tablespoon of flax meal

1 cup of water

1 freshly chopped sprig of fresh rosemary

½ teaspoon of Italian seasoning

½ freshly sliced red onion

¼ teaspoon of baking powder

Nutrition:

Fat: 8.5 g

Carbohydrate: 8.1 g

Protein: 7.5 g

Directions:

In a bowl, combine all the dry ingredients.

Chop the onion and zucchini.

Grate the cauliflower so that it has a rice-like consistency, and add it to the dry ingredients. Now, add the water and mix well.

Add the zucchini, onion, and rosemary last. You will have a clumpy and thick mixture, but you should be able to spoon it into a tin.

You can use either a silicone or a metal cake tin with a removable bottom. Now put the mixture in the tin and press it down gently.

The top should be left messy to resemble a rough texture.

Bake at 350o F for about half an hour. You will know your quiche is ready when the top is golden.

You can serve the quiche warm or cold, as per your preference.

Tasty Oatmeal and Carrot Cake

Servings: 2

Calories: 210

Preparation Time: 10 minutes

Cooking Time: 10 minutes

Ingredients:

1 cup of water

½ teaspoon of cinnamon

1 cup of rolled oats

Salt

¼ cup of raisins

½ cup of shredded carrots

1 cup of non-dairy milk

¼ teaspoon of allspice

½ teaspoon of vanilla extract

Toppings:

¼ cup of chopped walnuts

2 tablespoons of maple syrup

2 tablespoons of shredded coconut

Nutrition:

Fat: 11.48 g

Carbohydrate: 10.37 g

Protein: 3.8 g

Directions:

Put a small pot on low heat and bring the non-dairy milk, oats, and water to a simmer.

Now, add the carrots, vanilla extract, raisins, salt, cinnamon and allspice. You need to simmer all of the ingredients, but do not forget to stir them. You will know that they are ready when the liquid is fully absorbed into all of the ingredients (in about 7-10 minutes).

Transfer the thickened dish to bowls. You can drizzle some maple syrup on top or top them with coconut or walnuts.

This nutritious bowl will allow you to kickstart your day.

Onion & Mushroom Tart with a Nice Brown Rice Crust

Servings: 6

Calories: 245.3

Preparation Time: 10 minutes

Cooking Time: 55 minutes

Ingredients:

1 ½ pounds of mushrooms: button, portabella, or shiitake

1 cup of short-grain brown rice

2 ¼ cups of water

½ teaspoon of ground black pepper

2 teaspoons of herbal spice blend

1 sweet large onion

7 ounces of extra-firm tofu

1 cup of plain non-dairy milk

2 teaspoons of onion powder

2 teaspoons of low-sodium soy or tamari sauce

1 teaspoon of molasses

¼ teaspoon of ground turmeric

¼ cup of white wine or cooking sherry

¼ cup of tapioca or arrowroot powder

Nutrition:

Fat: 16.4 g

Protein: 6.8 g

Carbohydrate: 18.3 g

Directions:

Cook the brown rice and put it aside for later use.

Slice the onions into thin strips and sauté them in water until they are soft. Then, add the molasses, and cook them for a few minutes.

Next, sauté the mushrooms in water with the herbal spice blend. Once the mushrooms are cooked and they are soft, add the white wine or sherry. Cook everything for a few more minutes.

In a blender, combine milk, tofu, arrowroot, turmeric, and onion powder till you have a smooth mixture

On a pie plate, create a layer of rice, spreading evenly to form a crust. The rice should be warm and not cold. It will be easy to work with warm rice. You can also use a pastry roller to get an even crust. With your fingers, gently press the sides.

Take half of the tofu mixture and the mushrooms and spoon them over the tart dish. Smooth the level with your spoon.

Now, top the layer with onions followed by the tofu mixture. You can smooth the surface again with your spoon.

Sprinkle some black pepper on top.

Bake the pie at 350o F for about 45 minutes. Toward the end, you can cover it loosely with tin foil. This will help the crust to remain moist.

Allow the pie crust to cool down, so that you can slice it. If you are in love with vegetarian dishes, there is no way that you will not love this pie.

If you have guests, they are sure to marvel at your amazing pie made of mushrooms with a fine brown rice crust.

Tasty Oatmeal Muffins

Servings: 12

Calories: 133

Preparation Time: 10 minutes

Cooking Time: 20 minutes

Ingredients:

½ cup of hot water

½ cup of raisins

¼ cup of ground flaxseed

2 cups of rolled oats

¼ teaspoon of sea salt

½ cup of walnuts

¼ teaspoon of baking soda

1 banana

2 tablespoons of cinnamon

¼ cup of maple syrup

Nutrition:

Fat: 2 g

Carbohydrates: 27 g

Protein: 3 g

Directions:

Whisk the flaxseed with water and allow the mixture to sit for about 5 minutes.

In a food processor, blend all the ingredients along with the flaxseed mix. Blend everything for 30 seconds, but do not create a smooth substance. To create rough-textured cookies, you need to have a semi-coarse batter.

Put the batter in cupcake liners and place them in a muffin tin. As this is an oil-free recipe, you will need cupcake liners. Bake everything for about 20 minutes at 350 degrees.

Enjoy the freshly-made cookies with a glass of warm milk.

Omelet with Chickpea Flour

Servings: 1

Calories: 150

Preparation Time: 10 minutes

Cooking Time: 20 minutes

Ingredients:

½ teaspoon of onion powder

¼ teaspoon of black pepper

1 cup of chickpea flour

½ teaspoon of garlic powder

½ teaspoon of baking soda

¼ teaspoon of white pepper

1/3 cup of nutritional yeast

3 finely chopped green onions

4 ounces of sautéed mushrooms

Nutrition:

Fat: 1.9 g

Carbohydrates: 24.4 g

Protein: 10.2 g

Directions:

In a small bowl, mix the onion powder, white pepper, chickpea flour, garlic powder, black and white pepper, baking soda, and nutritional yeast. Add 1 cup of water and create a smooth batter.

On medium heat, put a frying pan and add the batter just like the way you would cook pancakes. On the batter, sprinkle some green onion and mushrooms. Flip the omelet and cook evenly on both sides.

Once both sides are cooked, serve the omelet with spinach, tomatoes, hot sauce, and salsa. Enjoy a guilt-free meal.

A Toast to Remember

Servings: 4

Calories: 290

Preparation Time: 10 minutes

Cooking Time: 15 minutes

Ingredients:

1 can of black beans

Pinch of sea salt

2 pieces of whole-wheat toast

¼ teaspoon of chipotle spice

Pinch of black pepper

1 teaspoon of garlic powder

1 freshly juiced lime

1 freshly diced avocado

¼ cup of corn

3 tablespoons of finely diced onion

½ freshly diced tomato

Fresh cilantro

Nutrition:

Fat: 9 g

Carbohydrates: 44 g

Protein: 12 g

Directions:

Mix the chipotle spice with the beans, salt, garlic powder, and pepper. Stir in the lime juice. Boil all of these until you have a thick and starchy mix.

In a bowl, mix the corn, tomato, avocado, red onion, cilantro, and juice from the rest of the lime. Add some pepper and salt.

Toast the bread and first spread the black bean mixture followed by the avocado mix.

Take a bite of wholesome goodness!

Tasty Panini

Servings: 1

Calories: 850

Preparation Time: 5 minutes

Ingredients:

¼ cup of hot water

1 tablespoon of cinnamon

¼ cup of raisins

2 teaspoons of cacao powder

1 ripe banana

2 slices of whole-grain bread

¼ cup of natural peanut butter

Nutrition:

Fat: 34 g Carbohydrates: 112 g Protein: 27 g

Directions: In a bowl, mix the cinnamon, hot water, raisins, and cacao powder.

Spread the peanut butter on the bread. Cut the bananas and put them on the toast. Mix the raisin mixture in a blender and spread it on the sandwich.

Amazing Blueberry Smoothie

Servings: 2

Calories: 220

Preparation Time: 5 minutes

Ingredients:

½ avocado

1 cup of frozen blueberries

1 cup of raw spinach

Pinch of sea salt

1 cup of soy or unsweetened almond milk

1 frozen banana

Nutrition:

Fat: 9 g

Carbohydrates: 32 g

Protein: 5 g

Directions:

Blend everything in a powerful blender until you have a smooth, creamy shake.

Enjoy your healthy shake and start your morning on a fresh note!

Chapter 11. Lunch Recipes

Stuffed Sweet Potatoes

Preparation Time: 30 minutes

Cooking time: 1 hour 16 minutes

Servings: 3

Ingredients:

½ cup dry black beans

3 small or medium sweet potatoes

2 tbsp. olive oil

1 large red bell pepper, pitted, chopped

1 large green bell pepper, pitted, chopped

1 small sweet yellow onion, chopped

2 tbsp. garlic, minced or powdered

1 8-oz. package tempeh, diced into ¼" cubes

½ cup marinara sauce

½ cup of water

1 tbsp chilli powder

1 tsp. parsley

½ tsp. cayenne

Salt and pepper to taste

Directions:

Preheat the oven to 400°F.

Use a fork to poke several holes in the skins of the sweet potatoes.

Wrap the sweet potatoes tightly with aluminium foil and place them in the oven until soft and tender, or for approximately 45 minutes.

While sweet potatoes are cooking, heat the olive oil in a deep pan over medium-high heat. Add the onions, bell peppers, and garlic; cook until the onions are tender, for about 10 minutes.

Add the water, together with the cooked beans, marinara sauce, chilli powder, parsley, and cayenne. Bring the mixture to a boil and then lower the heat to medium or low. Simmer for about 15 minutes, until the liquid has thickened.

Add the diced tempeh cubes and heat until warmed, around 1 minute.

Blend in salt and pepper to taste.

When the potatoes are done baking, remove them from the oven. Cut a slit across the top of each one, but do not split the potatoes all the way in half.

Top each potato with a scoop of the beans, vegetables, and tempeh mixture. Place the filled potatoes back in the hot oven for about 5 minutes. Serve after cooling for a few minutes, or, store for another day!

Nutritional value per serving: Calories: 498, Carbs: 55.7 g, Fat: 17.1 g, Protein: 20.7 g.

Vegan Mac and Cheese

Preparation Time: 10 minutes
Cooking time: 30 minutes
Servings: 4

Ingredients

6 oz. cooked whole-grain macaroni elbows

1 ½ cups broccoli, cooked lightly

1 ½ tbsps. extra-virgin olive oil

1 chopped yellow onion,

1 medium potato, grated

2 minced cloves garlic

½ tsp garlic powder

½ tsp onion powder

½ tsp mustard powder

½ tsp salt

¼ tsp red pepper flakes

½ cup raw cashews

1 cup of water

¼ cup nutritional yeast

2 tsp apple cider vinegar

Directions:

Soak the cashews in hot water for at least 4 hours

Place the cooked broccoli and pasta into a large bowl.

Pop a large saucepan over medium heat and add the oil.

Add the onion and sauté for 6 minutes until soft.

Add a pinch of salt, the potato, garlic, garlic powder, onion, onion powder, mustard powder and red pepper flakes. Stir well then leave to cook for another minute.

Add the cashews and water and stir. Simmer for 5-8 minutes until the potatoes have cooked.

Pour into a blender, add the nutritional yeast and vinegar and whizz until smooth.

Slowly add the water to the sauce reaches your desired consistency.

Pour over the pasta and broccoli, stir well then enjoy.

Nutritional value per serving: Calories: 506, Carbs: 58g, Fat: 21g, Protein: 18g

Satay Tempeh with Cauliflower Rice

Preparation Time: 60 minutes

Cooking time: 15 minutes

Servings: 4

Ingredients:

¼ cup water

4 tbsp. peanut butter

3 tbsp. low sodium soy sauce

2 tbsp. coconut sugar

1 garlic clove, minced

½-inch ginger, minced

2 tsp. rice vinegar

1 tsp. red pepper flakes

4 tbsp. olive oil

2 8-oz. packages tempeh, drained

2 cups cauliflower rice

1 cup purple cabbage, diced

1 tbsp. sesame oil

1 tsp. agave nectar

Directions:

In a large bowl, combine the sauce ingredients and then whisk until the mixture is smooth and any lumps have dissolved.

Cut the tempeh into ½-inch cubes and put them into the sauce, stirring to make sure the cubes get coated thoroughly.

Place the bowl in the refrigerator to marinate the tempeh for up to 3 hours.

Before the tempeh is done marinating, preheat the oven to 400°F.

Spread the tempeh out in one layer on a baking sheet lined with parchment paper or lightly greased with olive oil.

Bake the marinated cubes until browned and crisp—about 15 minutes.

Heat the cauliflower rice in a saucepan with 2 tablespoons of olive oil over medium heat until it is warm.

Rinse the large bowl with water, and then mix the cabbage, sesame oil, and agave together.

Serve a scoop of the cauliflower rice topped with the marinated cabbage and cooked tempeh on a plate and enjoy. Or, store for later.

Nutritional value per serving: Calories: 531, Carbs: 31.7 g, Fat: 33 g, Protein: 27.6 g.

Sweet Potato Quesadillas

Preparation Time: 30 minutes

Cooking time: 1 hour 9 minutes

Servings: 3

Ingredients:

1 cup dry black beans

½ cup dry rice of choice

1 large sweet potato, peeled and diced

½ cup of salsa

3-6 tortilla wraps

1 tbsp. olive oil

½ tsp. garlic powder

½ tsp. onion powder

½ tsp. paprika

Directions:

Preheat the oven to 350°F.

Line a baking pan with parchment paper.

Drizzle olive oil on the sweet potato cubes. Transfer the cubes to the baking pan.

Bake the potatoes in the oven until tender, for around 1 hour.

Allow about 5 minutes for the potatoes to cool and then add them to a large mixing bowl with the salsa and cooked rice. Use a fork to mash the ingredients together into a thoroughly combined mixture.

Heat a saucepan over medium-high heat and add the potato/rice mixture, cooked black beans, and spices to the pan.

Cook everything for about 5 minutes or until it is heated through.

Take another frying pan and put it over medium-low heat. Place a tortilla in the pan and fill half of it with a heaping scoop of the potato, bean, and rice mixture.

Fold the tortilla halfway to cover the filling and cook until both sides are browned— about 4 minutes per side.

Serve the tortillas with some additional salsa on the side.

Nutritional value per serving: Calories: 329, Carbs: 54.8 g, Fat: 7.5 g, Protein: 10.6 g.

Spicy Grilled Tofu with Szechuan Vegetables

Preparation Time: 3 minutes

Cooking time: 12 minutes

Servings: 2

Ingredients

1 lb. firm tofu, frozen and thawed

3 tablespoons soy sauce

2 tablespoons toasted sesame oil

2 tablespoons apple cider vinegar

1 clove garlic, minced

1 teaspoon freshly grated ginger

¼ teaspoon red pepper flakes

For the vegetables…

1 tablespoon toasted sesame oil

1 lb. fresh green beans, trimmed

1 red bell pepper, sliced

1 small red onion, sliced

1 teaspoon soy sauce

2 tablespoons Szechuan sauce

1 teaspoon corn starch

Directions:

Start by cutting the tofu into ½" slices then place into a shallow baking dish.

Take a small bowl and add the marinade ingredients. Stir well then pour over the tofu.

Put in a refrigerator for at least 30 minutes.

Preheat the broiler to medium then grill the tofu until firm.

Fill a pot with water and pop over medium heat.

Bring to the boil then add the beans.

Blanche for 2 minutes then drain and rinse.

Take a small bowl and add the corn starch and a teaspoon of cold water.

Place a skillet over medium heat, add the oil then add the beans, red peppers and onions. Stir well.

Add the soy sauce and Szechuan sauce and cook for another minute.

Add the corn starch mixture and stir again.

Serve the veggies and the tofu together.

Nutritional value per serving: Calories: 297, Carbs: 9g, Fat: 20g, Protein: 24g

Vegan-Friendly Fajitas

Preparation Time: 30 minutes

Cooking time: 19 minutes

Servings: 6

Ingredients:

1 cup dry black beans

1 large green bell pepper, seeded, diced

1 poblano pepper, seeded, thinly sliced

1 large avocado, peeled, pitted, mashed

1 medium sweet onion, chopped

3 large portobello mushrooms

2 tbsp. olive oil

6 tortilla wraps

1 tsp. lime juice

1 tsp. chilli powder

1 tsp. garlic powder

¼ tsp. cayenne pepper

Salt to taste

Directions:

Cook the black beans as recommended.

Heat 1 tablespoon of olive oil in a large frying pan over high heat.

Add the bell peppers, poblano peppers, and half of the onions.

Mix in the chilli powder, garlic powder, and cayenne pepper; add salt to taste.

Cook the vegetables until tender and browned, around 10 minutes.

Add the black beans and continue cooking for an additional 2 minutes; then remove the frying pan from the stove.

Add the portobello mushrooms to the skillet and turn the heat down to low. Sprinkle the mushrooms with salt.

Stir/flip the ingredients often and cook until the mushrooms have shrunk down to half their size, around 7 minutes. Remove the frying pan from the heat.

Mix the avocado, remaining 1 tablespoon of olive oil, and the remaining onions together in a small bowl to make a simple guacamole. Stir the lime juice in and add salt and pepper to taste. Spread the guacamole on a tortilla with a spoon and then top with a generous scoop of the mushroom mixture.Serve and enjoy right away, or, allow the prepared tortillas to cool down and wrap them in paper towels to store!

Nutritional value per serving: Calories: 264, Carbs: 27.7 g, Fat: 14 g. Protein: 6.8 g

Incredibly Tasty Pizza

Preparation time: 1 hour and 10 minutes

Cooking time: 1 hour and 45 minutes

Servings: 3

Ingredients:

For the dough:

½ Teaspoon italian seasoning

1 and ½ cups whole wheat flour

1 and ½ teaspoons instant yeast

1 tablespoon olive oil

A pinch of salt

½ Cup warm water

Cooking spray

For the sauce:

¼ Cup green olives, pitted and sliced

¼ Cup kalamata olives, pitted and sliced

½ Cup tomatoes, crushed

1 tablespoon parsley, chopped

1 tablespoon capers, rinsed

¼ Teaspoon garlic powder

¼ Teaspoon basil, dried

¼ Teaspoon oregano, dried

¼ Teaspoon palm sugar

¼ Teaspoon red pepper flakes

A pinch of salt and black pepper

½ Cup cashew mozzarella, shredded

Directions:

In your food processor, mix yeast with italian seasoning, a pinch of salt and flour. Add oil and the water and blend well until you obtain a dough. Transfer dough to a floured working surface, knead well, transfer to a greased bowl, cover and leave aside for 1 hour. Meanwhile, in a bowl, mix green olives with kalamata olives, tomatoes, parsley, capers, garlic powder, oregano, sugar, salt, pepper and pepper flakes and stir well. Transfer pizza dough to a working surface again and flatten it. Shape so it will fit your slow cooker. Grease your slow cooker with cooking spray and add dough.

Press well on the bottom. Spread the sauce mix all over, cover and cook on high for 1 hour and 15 minutes. Spread vegan mozzarella all over, cover again and cook on high for 30 minutes more. Leave your pizza to cool down before slicing and serving it.

Nutrition: calories 340, fat 5, fiber 7, carbs 13, protein 15

Rich Beans Soup

Preparation time: 10 minutes

Cooking time: 7 hours

Servings: 4

Ingredients:

1 pound navy beans

1 yellow onion, chopped

4 garlic cloves, crushed, 2 quarts veggie stock

A pinch of sea salt

Black pepper to the taste

2 potatoes, peeled and cubed

2 teaspoons dill, dried

1 cup sun-dried tomatoes, chopped

1 pound carrots, sliced

4 tablespoons parsley, minced

Directions: Put the stock in your slow cooker. Add beans, onion, garlic, potatoes, tomatoes, carrots, dill, salt and pepper, stir, cover and cook on low for 7 hours. Stir your soup, add parsley, divide into bowls and serve. Enjoy!

Nutrition: calories 250, fat 4, fiber 3, carbs 9, protein 10

Delicious Baked Beans

Preparation time: 10 minutes

Cooking time: 12 hours

Servings: 8

Ingredients:

1 pound navy beans, soaked overnight and drained

1 cup maple syrup

1 cup bourbon

1 cup vegan bbq sauce

1 cup palm sugar

¼ Cup ketchup

1 cup water

¼ Cup mustard, ¼ Cup blackstrap molasses

¼ Cup apple cider vinegar, ¼ Cup olive oil

2 tablespoons coconut aminos

Directions: Put the beans in your slow cooker. Add maple syrup, bourbon, bbq sauce, sugar, ketchup, water, mustard, molasses, vinegar, oil and coconut aminos. Stir everything, cover and cook on Low for 12 hours. Divide into bowls and serve. Enjoy!

Nutrition: calories 430, fat 7, fiber 8, carbs 15, protein 19

Indian Lentils

Preparation time: 10 minutes

Cooking time: 3 hours

Servings: 4

Ingredients:

1 yellow bell pepper, chopped

1 sweet potato, chopped

2 and ½ cups lentils, already cooked

4 garlic cloves, minced

1 yellow onion, chopped

2 teaspoons cumin, ground

15 ounces canned tomato sauce

½ Teaspoon ginger, ground

A pinch of cayenne pepper

1 tablespoons coriander, ground

1 teaspoon turmeric, ground

2 teaspoons paprika

2/3 cup veggie stock

1 teaspoon garam masala

A pinch of sea salt

Black pepper to the taste

Juice of 1 lemon

Directions:

Put the stock in your slow cooker.

Add potato, lentils, onion, garlic, cumin, bell pepper, tomato sauce, salt, pepper, ginger, coriander, turmeric, paprika, cayenne, garam masala and lemon juice.

Stir, cover and cook on high for 3 hours.

Stir your lentils mix again, divide into bowls and serve.

Enjoy!

Nutrition: calories 300, fat 6, fiber 5, carbs 9, protein 12

Delicious Butternut Squash Soup

Preparation time: 10 minutes

Cooking time: 6 hours

Servings: 8

Ingredients:

1 apple, cored, peeled and chopped

½ Pound carrots, chopped

1 pound butternut squash, peeled and cubed

1 yellow onion, chopped

A pinch of sea salt

Black pepper to the taste

1 bay leaf

3 cups veggie stock

14 ounces canned coconut milk

¼ Teaspoon sage, dried

Directions: Put the stock in your slow cooker. Add apple squash, carrots, onion, salt, pepper and bay leaf. Stir, cover and cook on low for 6 hours. Transfer to your blender, add coconut milk and sage and pulse really well. Ladle into bowls and serve right away. Enjoy!

Nutrition: calories 200, fat 3, fiber 6, carbs 8, protein 10

Chapter 12. Dinner Recipes

Black Bean and Veggie Soup

Servings: 6

Calories: 308

Preparation Time: 10 minutes

Cooking Time: 45 minutes

Ingredients

Olive oil - 2 tablespoons

Onion (diced) - 1

Celery stalks (chopped) - 2

Carrot (chopped) - 1

Red bell pepper (diced) - 1

Garlic (minced) - 4 cloves

Jalapeño (seeded and diced) - 1

Salt - 1 teaspoon

Pepper - 1 teaspoon

Cumin - 2 tablespoons

Black beans (drained and rinsed) – 4 cans (60 ounces)

Vegetable stock - 4 cups

Bay leaf – 1

For serving

Avocado (chopped)

Queso fresco (crumbled)

Fresh cilantro (chopped)

Tortilla chip (crumbled)

Nutrition:

Fat: 6 g

Carbohydrates: 49 g

Protein: 17 g

Directions

Start by taking a stock-pot (large) and place it over high flame. Add in the oil and reduce the heat the medium–high.

Once the oil starts to shimmer, toss in the onions, carrot, bell peppers and celery.

Let the veggies cook for about 5 minutes. Keep stirring.

Now add in the minced garlic, pepper and salt. Cook for about 10 more minutes. The veggies should be tender by now.

Add in the vegetable stock, black beans, bay leaf and cumin.

Bring the ingredients to a boil and reduce the flame to low. Cover the stock-pot with a lid and cook for about 30 minutes. Beans should also be tender by now.

Take a blender and transfer 4 cups of the beans and vegetable soup into the same. Blend into a smooth puree like consistency.

Pour the blended vegetables and beans into the stock-pot. Mix well to combine. This will help in thickening the soup.

Let the soup simmer over low flame for another 10 minutes.

Once done, garnish with queso fresco, avocado, tortilla chips and chopped cilantro.

Vegetable and Tofu Skewers

Servings: 4

Calories: 187

Preparation Time: 10 minutes (1 hour additional)

Cooking Time: 17 minutes

Ingredients

Water - ½ cup

Maple syrup - ¼ cup

Soy sauce - 3 tablespoons

BBQ sauce - 2 tablespoons

Oil - 1 tablespoon

Garlic powder - 1 tablespoon

Sriracha - 1 tablespoon

Black pepper - 1 teaspoon

Firm tofu - 15 ounces

Peppers - 2

Onions – 2 medium

Zucchini - 1

Skewers - 4

Nutrition:

Fat: 9 g

Carbohydrates: 17 g

Protein: 11 g

Directions

Start by taking a shallow dish and fill it with water. Soak the wooden skewers in the same as this will prevent them from burning.

Take the zucchini and slice it in round slices. Also cut peppers and onions in squares.

In the meanwhile, take a quarter plate and line it with a paper towel. Place tofu and cover it with another paper towel and place a plate on top.

Place the tofu along with plates in the microwave for about 3 minutes.

Remove the tofu and place it on a chopping board. Cut it into cubes.

Take a glass measuring cup and add in the water, soy sauce, maple syrup, oil, barbeque sauce, pepper, Sriracha and garlic powder. Stir well.

Take a rectangle storage box and place the tofu inside it. Pour the prepared sauce over tofu and cover it with a lid. Place it in the refrigerator for about an hour.

Once done, remove the tofu from marinade. Keep aside

Take a non-stick saucepan and pour the marinating liquid to the saucepan. Place it over low flame for about 10 minutes. Put off the flame once the sauce starts to thicken.

Remove the skewers from the water and start assembling them.

Take 1 skewer and start assembling by alternating between zucchini, onion, pepper and tofu.

Take a grill pan and place in medium flame. Cook each assembled skewer on each side for about 4 minutes. Glaze each side with sauce while cooking.

All sides should have a light char as this will add nice smoky flavor to the dish.

Vegan Alfredo Fettuccine Pasta

Servings: 2

Calories: 844

Preparation Time: 15 minutes

Cooking Time: 15 minutes

Ingredients

White potatoes - 2 medium

White onion - ¼

Italian seasoning - 1 tablespoon

Lemon juice - 1 teaspoon

Garlic - 2 cloves

Salt - 1 teaspoon

Fettuccine pasta - 12 ounces

Raw cashew - ½ cup

Nutritional yeast (optional) - 1 teaspoon

Truffle oil (optional) - ¼ teaspoon

Nutrition:

Fat: 13 g

Carbohydrates: 152 g

Protein: 28 g

Directions

Start by placing a pot on high flame and boiling 4 cups of water.

Peel the potatoes and cut them into small cubes. Cut the onion into cubes as well.

Add the potatoes and onions to the boiling water and cook for about 10 minutes.

Remove the onions and potatoes. Keep aside. Save the water.

Take another pot and fill it with water. Season generously with salt.

Toss in the fettuccine pasta and cook as per package instructions.

Take a blender and add in the raw cashews, veggies, nutritional yeast, truffle oil, lemon juice and 1 cup of saved water. Blend into a smooth puree.

Add in the garlic and salt.

Drain the cooked pasta using a colander. Transfer into a mixing bowl.

Pour the prepared sauce on top of the cooked fettuccine pasta. Serve.

Spinach Pasta in Pesto Sauce

Servings: 2

Calories: 591

Preparation Time: 20 minutes

Cooking Time: 15 minutes

Ingredients

Olive oil - 1 tablespoon

Spinach - 5 ounces

All-purpose flour - 2 cups

Salt - 1 tablespoon plus ¼ teaspoon (keep it divided)

Water - 2 tablespoons

Roasted vegetable for serving

Pesto for serving

Fresh basil for serving

Nutrition:

Fat: 8 g

Carbohydrates: 110 g

Protein: 16 g

Directions

Take a large pot and fill it with water. Place it over high flame and bring the water to a boil. Add one tablespoon of salt

While the water is boiling, place a large saucepan over medium flame. Pour in the olive oil and heat it through.

Once the oil starts to shimmer, toss in the spinach and sauté for 5 minutes.

Take a food processor and transfer the wilted spinach. Process until the spinach is fine in texture.

Add in the flour bit by bit and continue to process to form a crumbly dough.

Further, add ¼ tsp of salt and 1 tbsp of water while processing to bring the dough together. Add the remaining 1 tbsp of water if required.

Remove the dough onto a flat surface and sprinkle with flour. Knead well to form a dough ball.Use a rolling pin to roll out the dough. The dimensions of the rolled dough should be 18 inches long and 12 inches wide. The thickness should be about ¼ - inch thick.Cut the rolled dough into long and even strips using a pizza cutter. Make sure the strips are ½ - inch wide. The strips need to be rolled into evenly sized thick noodles.Toss in the prepared noodles and cook for about 4 minutes. Drain using a colander.Transfer the noodles into a large mixing bowl and add in the roasted vegetables, pesto. Toss well to combine.Garnish with basil leaves.

No Meat Sloppy Joes

Servings: 4

Calories: 451

Preparation Time: 10 minutes

Cooking Time: 24 minutes

Ingredients

Olive oil – ½ teaspoon

Yellow onion (diced) - ½ medium

Green capsicum (diced) - ½

Garlic (minced) - 2 cloves

Chili powder - ½ teaspoon

Cumin - ½ teaspoon

Paprika - ½ teaspoon

Salt – as per taste

Textured vegetable protein - 1 cup

Vegetable broth - 1 cup

Tomato sauce - 1 can (15 ounces)

Vegan Worcestershire sauce - 1 teaspoon

Soy sauce - 1 tablespoon

Brown sugar - 1 teaspoon

Yellow mustard - 2 teaspoons

Hamburger buns - 4

Nutrition:

Fat: 10 g

Carbohydrates: 61 g

Protein: 27 g

Directions

Start by taking a medium-sized skillet and place it over medium flame. Pour olive oil and heat through.

Once the oil is heated, add in the diced onions and sauté for 3 minutes.

Now toss in the diced capsicum and sauté for 3 more minutes.

Add in the garlic, cumin, chili powder, salt and paprika and sauté for another 3 minutes.

Add in the vegetable protein, tomato sauce and vegetable broth. Stir well to combine. Cover with a lid and let it cook for about 15 minutes.

Open the lid and keep on the side. Add in the soy sauce, Worcestershire sauce, yellow mustard and brown sugar. Mix well. Cook for about 4 minutes. Place the prepared mixture between the hamburger buns and serve hot!

Acorn Squash Stuffed with Veggies and Wild Rice

Servings: 2

Calories: 409

Preparation Time: 10 minutes

Cooking Time: 1 hour 40 minutes

Ingredients

Acorn squashes - 2

Olive oil - 1 tablespoon (some extra)

Salt – as per taste

Pepper – as per taste

Wild rice (rinsed) - ¾ cup

Vegetable broth - 1 ¼ cups (2 tablespoons extra, divided)

Chili powder - ½ teaspoon

Ground cumin - ¼ teaspoon

Maple syrup - 1 ½ teaspoon

Cremini mushroom (sliced) - 5 ounces

Shiitake mushroom (sliced) – 5 ounces

Onion (chopped) - ½ medium

Garlic (minced) - 2 cloves

Fresh rosemary (chopped) - 1 teaspoon

Fresh thyme (chopped) - 1 teaspoon

White wine - ¼ cup

Kale (chopped) - 2 cups

Pomegranate seeds - 2 tablespoons

Nutrition:

Fat: 5 g

Carbohydrates: 88 g

Protein: 13 g

Directions

Start by preheating the oven by setting the temperature to 375 degrees Fahrenheit.

Place the squash on the chopping board and cut in half from stem side up. Remove the seeds and keep aside. Scoop out the pulp into a bowl and keep aside.

Place the squash on a baking tray with cut-side facing up. Brush the squash with oil and evenly sprinkle with pepper and salt.

Transfer into the oven and bake for about 40 minutes.

While the squash is cooking, take a small stockpot and add in 1 ¼ cups of vegetable broth. Let it come to a boil. Cover using a lid and let it simmer for about 45 minutes over low flame.

Place the squash seeds in a strainer and rinse them thoroughly. Dry them using a dishtowel.

Transfer the seeds into a small bowl. Add in the cumin, chili powder, maple syrup and salt. Toss well to until all seeds are evenly coated.

Remove the baking tray from the oven and shift the squash to one side. Make a shallow tray using the parchment paper. Place the seeds in the same and transfer back into the oven.

Bake for about 15 minutes. The squash should be tender and seeds should be crispy.

Take a large skillet and add in the olive oil. Place it over medium flame.

Once the oil is heated through, toss in the mushrooms and sauté for about 8 minutes.

Toss in the onions and sauté for about 4 minutes. Further, drizzle some olive oil and add in the rosemary, thyme and garlic. Cook for about 4 minutes. Pour in the white wine to deglaze the skillet. Cook for about 2 minutes. Add in the kale, pepper and salt. Sauté until kale starts wilting and reduces to a quarter of the volume. Add in the wild rice and mix through. Remove the skillet from the flame and keep aside.

Place both squashes on serving platter and fill them with kale and mushroom mixture. Garnish with pomegranate seeds and crispy squash seeds.

Tofu Turkey and Drumsticks

Servings: 6

Calories: 339

Preparation Time: 20 minutes

Cooking Time: 1 hour

Ingredients

Extra-firm tofu - 14 ounces

Pinto bean - ¾ cup

Nutritional yeast - 6 tablespoons

Soy sauce - ¼ cup

Poultry seasoning - 1 tablespoon

Garlic (chopped) - 3 cloves

Kosher salt - ½ teaspoon

Pepper - 1 teaspoon

Onion powder - 1 teaspoon

Vegetable broth (low sodium) - 1 cup

Olive oil - 2 tablespoons

Vital wheat gluten - 2 ½ cups

Vegan stuffing - ½ cup

Wooden skewers – 2

Gravy (of choice) - for serving

Nutrition:

Fat: 9 g

Carbohydrates: 18 g

Protein: 47 g

Directions

Start by preheating the oven by setting the temperature to 375 degrees Fahrenheit.

Take a shallow dish and fill it with water. Soak the skewers in the same.

Take a medium-sized bowl and line it with a kitchen towel. Crumble the tofu in the bowl. Gather all the edges of the kitchen towel and press through the center to squeeze out excess liquid.

Take a food processor and add in the drained tofu, pinto beans, soy sauce, nutritional yeast, onion powder, poultry seasoning, pepper, salt, vegetable broth and onion powder. Blend into a smooth puree like consistency. While the processor is running, add in the olive oil. Make sure all ingredients are well incorporated.

Take a large bowl and add in the wheat gluten. Now transfer the prepared puree from the food processor to the same bowl. Stir well to combine all the ingredients together. Knead into a smooth dough and transfer onto a flat surface. Form a ball.

Cut out a quarter of the dough and keep aside.

Place the rest of the dough into a glass bowl. Make a well into the center by stretching the edges. It needs to be expanded to about 4 inches in diameter.

Place the vegetable stuffing in the well and enclose the well by stretching the edges.

Take a parchment paper and nicely wrap the dough. Also, wrap the dough in a foil.

Take the saved dough and divide in two equal halves. Form the dough in the shape of drumsticks. Insert soaked skewers in both the drumsticks. Wrap both the drumsticks nice with parchment paper and then in foil. Enclose the edges nicely.

Take a baking tray and place both drumsticks and tofu turkey. Bake for about 20 minutes and flip over. Bake for another 20 minutes and flip over again. Remove the drumsticks after 40 minutes.

Bake the tofu turkey for 20 more minutes.

Once done, remove from the oven and transfer the drumsticks and tofu turkey onto a wooden chopping block. Remove the foil and parchment paper.

Place onto a serving platter and serve with your choice of gravy.

Chapter 13. Snacks And Salad Recipes

Energy Bars

Preparation Time: 5 minutes

Cooking Time: 20 minutes

Servings: Makes 12 bars

Ingredients:

½ cup raisins

1 cup desiccated coconut

1 tsp. vanilla extract

½ cup hemp seeds, shelled

1 tsp. cinnamon, ground

½ cup sesame seeds

4 tbsp. maple syrup

½ cup pumpkin seeds

½ cup cashew butter or any nut butter

1 ½ cup mixed nuts, chopped

1 tsp. vanilla extract

Directions:

First preheat the oven to 350°F.

Mix the coconut, cinnamon, nuts and raisin in a medium-sized mixing bowl.

Add the cashew butter and maple syrup to a small saucepan and heat it over medium heat until melted and smooth.

Stir in the vanilla extract.

Pour the cashew butter mixture into the mixing bowl and stir until everything comes together. Tip: Add water if needed to help the mixture come together.

Transfer the mixture to a greased baking tin and press it down into the tin so it is evenly spread.

Bake for 13 to 15 minutes or until golden brown.

Allow the bars to cool completely and slice them into bars. Store in an air-tight container.

Tip: You can add toppings like walnuts and pecan.

Nutrition:

Calories: 340Kcal

Protein: 10g

Carbohydrates: 20.8g

Fat: 24.4g

Vegan Muffins

Preparation Time: 5 minutes

Cooking Time: 25 minutes

Servings: 6

Ingredients:

1 oz. protein powder

1 tsp. baking powder

2 tbsp. pumpkin seeds

2 tbsp. dried cherries

1 cup oats

1 tbsp. sesame seeds, roasted

For the wet ingredients:

3 tbsp. olive oil

½ cup almond milk

1/2 cup apple sauce

Directions:

Preheat the oven to 390°F.

Combine all the dry ingredients into a large mixing bowl until mixed well.

Next, mix all the wet ingredients in another bowl and combine well.

Pour the wet ingredients into the dry and whisk until everything comes together.

Transfer the mixture to a greased and lined baking dish.

Finally, bake for 28 to 30 minutes or until they are golden brown.

Cool the muffins on the rack, then enjoy.

Tip: You could top the muffins with pumpkin seeds for a crunchy topping.

Nutrition:

Calories: 244Kcal

Protein: 11g

Carbohydrates: 24g

Fat: 13g

Cacao Walnut Balls

Preparation Time: 5 minutes

Cooking Time: 25 minutes

Servings: 6

Ingredients:

1 cup quinoa flour
1 cup walnut, halved
½ cup coconut flakes
3 tbsp. cacao powder
1 oz. protein powder, unflavored
1 cup coconut flakes
Pinch of sea salt
¼ cup dried apricots, chopped thinly

Directions:

Place all the ingredients, apart from the coconut flakes, into a large mixing bowl. Once everything is well combined, shape pieces of the mixture into balls and then coat each ball with coconut flakes.

Finally, place the balls in the refrigerator for a few hours and serve them chilled.

Tip: These balls are freezer friendly and can stay frozen for up to 2 months.

Nutrition: Calories: 343Kcal Protein: 12g Carbohydrates: 26g Fat: 24g

Almond Oats Energy Balls

Preparation Time: 5 minutes

Cooking Time: 25 minutes

Servings: 8

Ingredients:

½ cup almonds, roasted & crushed

1 cup oats

½ cup coconut milk

2 medium bananas

2 oz. protein powder

2 tbsp. chia seeds

1 tsp. cinnamon, ground

2 tbsp. cocoa or coconut flakes

Directions:

Combine the chia seeds and coconut milk in a large mixing bowl.

Set aside for 5 minutes and then stir in the rest of the ingredients. Mix well.

Transfer the mixture to a high-speed blender. Blend for ½ minutes or until it is just combined.

Put the mixture into the freezer for 10 minutes to chill it.

Next, shape the mixture into balls and dip them in cocoa powder.

Serve them chilled.

Tip: If you prefer, you can use your choice of low-carb sweetener.

Nutrition: Calories: 224Kcal Protein: 13g Carbohydrates: 24g Fat: 10g

Spicy Chickpeas

Preparation Time: 10 minutes

Cooking Time: 35 minutes

Servings: 6

Ingredients:

¼ cup olive oil

½ tsp. cayenne pepper

2 × 15 oz. chickpeas

¾ tsp. paprika

1 tsp. sea salt

½ tsp. chili powder

½ tsp. onion powder

½ tsp. cumin

Sea salt, as needed

¾ tsp. garlic powder

Directions: Preheat the oven to 425°F. Drain the chickpeas and let them dry in a towel-lined dish for 10 to 15 minutes.Transfer the chickpeas onto a lined baking sheet and spread them out in a single layer .Drizzle olive oil over the chickpeas and sprinkle with salt. Bake them in the oven for 23 to 25 minutes or until they are golden brown, stirring frequently. Once baked, stir in the remaining spices and toss well. Next, season and taste, adding more salt and pepper as needed. Serve and enjoy.Tip: You can also reduce the quantity of cayenne pepper to ¼ tsp.

Nutrition: Calories: 224Kcal Protein: 13g Carbohydrates: 24g Fat: 10g

Peanut Butter Cups

Preparation Time: 10 minutes

Cooking Time: 35 minutes

Servings: 9

Ingredients:

2 tsp. coconut oil

1 cup peanut butter, creamy

10 Oz. vegan, sugar-free chocolate chips

3 scoops chocolate protein powder

2 tbsp. maple syrup

Directions:

To begin, combine the peanut butter, protein powder and maple syrup in a large mixing bowl until mixed well.

Next, place the coconut oil and chocolate chips in a microwave-safe bowl and melt the mixture by heating it on a high heat.

Spoon the chocolate mixture into the bottom of the greased baking cups.

Add the peanut butter mixture on top of the chocolate mixture.

Finally, add the remaining chocolate on top of the peanut butter.

Place them in the refrigerator until set.

Serve and enjoy.

Tip: Make sure to add organic coconut oil.

Nutrition: Calories: 341Kcal Protein: 11.6g Carbohydrates: 30.4g Fat: 22.4g

Coleslaw Pasta Salad

Preparation Time: 5 minutes

Cooking Time: 30 minutes

Servings: 4

Ingredients:

4 scallions, sliced thinly

10 oz. pasta

1 lb. carrot, shredded

1 lb. white cabbage, shredded

For the dressing:

1 tsp. sea salt

½ cup vegan mayonnaise

1/2 tsp. black pepper, ground

2 tbsp. maple syrup

½ cup hummus

Juice of ½ of 1 lemon

2 tbsp. dijon mustard

Directions: Start by cooking the pasta, following the instructions given in the packet. Cook until al dente then drain. After that, make the dressing by placing all the ingredients in a medium bowl until combined well. Add the pasta along with the remaining ingredients. Spoon the dressing over it and toss well. Serve and enjoy. Tip: You could add nuts like walnuts to it to make the salad more nutritious.

Nutrition: Calories: 524Kcal Protein: 17g Carbohydrates: 85g Fat: 14g

Corn Avocado Salad

Preparation Time: 10 minutes

Cooking Time: 15 minutes

Servings: 4

Ingredients:

1 cup frozen edamame, unshelled, 2 avocadoes, sliced

1 medium shallot, sliced thinly

2 cups cherry tomatoes, halved

2 cups sweet corn kernels, frozen

For the dressing:

Juice of 1 lime

¼ tsp. chili powder

1 tsp. sea salt

1 tsp. extra virgin olive oil

¼ cup fresh cilantro, sliced thinly

Directions: Boil water in a medium-sized saucepan over a medium-high heat. Once it starts boiling, stir in the corn and simmer them for 6 to 8 minutes or until cooked. Tip: Make sure to not overcook. Drain. Transfer to a large mixing bowl and allow it to cool. Mix all the dressing ingredients in another bowl until combined well. Then add the rest of the ingredients along with dressing to the mixing bowl and toss well. Taste for seasoning and add more salt and pepper if needed. Serve and enjoy. Tip: Pair it with toasted whole-grain bread.

Nutrition: Calories: 375Kcal Protein: 14g Carbohydrates: 43g Fat: 20g

Couscous with Chickpeas Salad

Preparation Time: 10 minutes

Cooking Time: 15 minutes

Servings: 4

Ingredients:

For the couscous:

1 cup couscous

1 ½ cup water

For the salad:

12 oz. tofu, extra-firm

1 medium shallot, sliced thinly

1 cup chickpeas, washed

½ tsp. turmeric powder

1 tbsp. olive oil

1 cucumber, diced

½ tsp. turmeric powder

1 cucumber, diced

4 tbsp. pine nuts

1 cup dill

For the dressing:

Dash of pepper, ground

1 tbsp. dijon mustard

1 tsp. sea salt

½ cup orange juice

Directions:

Boil water in a pot over medium-high heat.

When it starts boiling, pour the hot water to a large heatproof bowl with couscous in it.

Cover the heatproof bowl with a lid and allow it to sit for 10 to 15 minutes or until all the liquid is absorbed.

Fluff the couscous with a fork.

Heat a skillet and spoon in 1/3 of the oil into it.

Then, stir in the sliced shallot and cook them for 3 minutes or until transparent. Set aside on a plate.

Add tofu to the skillet along with the remaining oil.

Fry the tofu for 8 to 10 minutes or until they are golden brown.

To this, add the turmeric powder and mix again.

In another bowl, stir in all the dressing ingredients until combined.

Finally, combine the couscous, salad ingredients and dressing in a large mixing bowl until mixed well.

Tip: Add a squeeze of lemon juice over as a finishing touch.

Nutrition:

Calories: 408Kcal

Protein: 18g

Carbohydrates: 54g

Fat: 14g

Black & White Bean Salad

Preparation Time: 10 minutes

Cooking Time: 15 minutes

Servings: 4

Ingredients:

For the salad:

¼ cup red onion, chopped

1/3 cup quinoa

1 cup cucumber, sliced

19 oz. drained black beans, washed

1 jalapeno pepper, seeded and minced

19 oz. drained navy beans, washed

¼ cup fresh coriander, chopped

For the dressing:

¼ tsp. pepper

¼ cup vegetable oil

¼ tsp. salt

2 tbsp. lime juice

½ tsp. chili powder

1 tsp. coriander, ground

1 tbsp. cider vinegar

½ tsp. oregano, dried

1 garlic clove, minced

Directions:

Cook the quinoa for 10 to 12 minutes in a deep saucepan filled with ¾ cup of water until it becomes tender.

Make the dressing by combining all the dressing ingredients in a small bowl until mixed well.

Finally, add all the salad ingredients to a large mixing bowl and stir in the cooked quinoa and dressing. Toss well.

Serve and enjoy.

Tip: Try adding tomato to the recipe.

Nutrition:

Calories: 573Kcal

Protein: 26.7g

Carbohydrates: 83.5g

Fat: 16.3g

Quinoa with Apple & Kale

Preparation Time: 10 minutes

Cooking Time: 25 minutes

Servings: 3

Ingredients:

5 cups kale

1 cup quinoa, washed

2 cloves of garlic, minced

1 tbsp. lemon juice

2 cups vegetable stock

Salt and pepper, as needed

2 tbsp. extra virgin olive oil

1 tbsp. coconut oil

1 tbsp. dijon mustard

1 large apple, diced

2 tbsp. maple syrup

3 tbsp. water

2 tbsp. apple cider vinegar

Chapter 14. Smoothies Recipes

Greens and Chocolate Protein Shake

Preparation Time: 70 minutes

Servings: 1

Ingredients:

¾ cup almond milk

2 large dates, pitted

1 tables poon cocoa powder

A pinch ground cinnamon

½ cup frozen organic kale

1 tablespoon hemp seeds, hulled

1 medium banana, sliced, frozen

1/8 cup chopped avocado

Ice cubes, as required

Directions:

Add all the ingredients into a blender. Blend for 30 – 40 seconds or until smooth. Pour into a glass and serve.

Nutrition: Calories: 250 Fat: 9 g
Carbohydrate: 38 g,Fiber: 8 g Protein: 10 g

Chocolate Black Bean Smoothie

Preparation Time: 40 minutes

Ingredients:

2 bananas, sliced, frozen

1 cup cooked black beans

2 cups almond milk or any other nondairy milk of your choice

2 tablespoons cocoa powder

2 cups frozen cauliflower

4 medjool dates, pitted, chopped

2 tablespoons hemp seeds

2 teaspoons ground cinnamon

To garnish:

Cocoa nibs (optional)

Directions:

Add all the ingredients into a blender. Blend for 30 – 40 seconds or until smooth.

Pour into 2 large glasses. Garnish with cocoa nibs and serve.

Nutrition: 2 large glasses Nutrition:
Calories: 452 Fat: 11 g Carbohydrate: 77 g, Fiber: 18 g Protein: 19 g

Peanut Butter Protein Smoothie

Preparation Time: 30 minutes

Servings: 1

Ingredients:

1 cup torn kale (discard hard stems and ribs)

1 tablespoon hemp seeds

1/3 cup water

½ cup almond milk or cashew milk

½ scoop vegan vanilla protein powder

½ banana, sliced

½ tablespoon peanut butter

1 cup ice

1 tablespoon cacao powder

Directions:

First add kale into the blender followed by banana, hemp seeds and peanut butter.

Add ice, water and almond milk and blend until smooth. Add rest of the ingredients and blend until smooth. Pour into a tall glass and serve.

Nutrition: Calories: 286 Fat: 11.6 g Carbohydrate: 27.9 g,

Fiber: 6 g Protein: 16.8 g

Peanut Butter, Jelly and Date Smoothie

Preparation Time: 20 minutes

Servings: 2

Ingredients:

8 dates, pitted

2 medium bananas, sliced, frozen

2/3 cup blueberries

2 tablespoons natural peanut butter

1 ½ cups vanilla almond milk, unsweetened

2 tablespoons flaxseed meal

Directions:

Place all the ingredients into a blender. Blend for 30 – 40 seconds or until smooth.

Pour into 2 glasses and serve.

Nutrition:
Calories: 374
Fat: 13 g Carbohydrate: 60 g,

Fiber: 11 g Protein: 8 g

Berry and Oatmeal Smoothie

Preparation Time: 20 minutes

Servings: 2 large glasses

Ingredients:

2 cups frozen strawberries

2 cups frozen blueberries

4 tablespoons maple syrup

4 tablespoons almond butter

2 inches fresh ginger, peeled, chopped

4 cups baby spinach

2 cups wate

6 tablespoons hulled hemp seeds

½ cup rolled oats

Directions:

Place all the ingredients into a blender. Blend for 30 – 40 seconds or until smooth.

Pour into 2 large glasses and serve.

Nutrition: Calories: 680

Fat: 36 g Carbohydrate: 84 g, Fiber: NA Protein: 21 g

Vanilla Clementine Protein Smoothie

Preparation Time: 70 minutes

Servings: 2

Ingredients:

6 clementine's, peeled, separated into segments, deseeded

2 cups light vanilla soymilk

16 almonds

1 scoop vegan vanilla protein powder

2 tablespoons flaxseed meal

Ice cubes, as required

Directions:

Place all the ingredients into a blender. Blend for 30 – 40 seconds or until smooth.

Pour into 2 glasses and serve.

Nutrition:
Calories: 336
Fat: 11.1 g
Carbohydrate: 39.8 g,
Fiber: 9.1 g
Protein: 27.3 g

Chapter 15. Don't Forget To Exercise

There are several things that you can do in order to meet your weight loss goals. These include cutting back on the number of calories that you eat each day and starting a healthy exercise program are two great ways to meet your goals, especially if you combine them both together. It is still important to maintain an exercise program even after you have reached your weight loss goals in order to maintain the weight loss. After you have decided to go on a diet and start an exercise program the first thing that you will be asking yourself is how much exercise that you will need.

An important step that you should consider doing before you start any exercise plan is to talk to your doctor. They will be able to tell you if the plan is good for you, how much exercise you should do, and give you any advice and suggestions about what will work in your situation. They will also be able to do a complete checkup in order to make sure that they are no underlying problems in your health that could affect what types of exercises you are able to do.

You should consider some basic considerations when you start a diet. It is important to remember that there are no magic pills or amazing diet plans that will help you to lose the weigh overnight. Even if you do lose a lot of weight quickly on a particular plan, it is not likely that you will be able to keep the weight off for the long term.

The easiest and safest way to lose weight is to combine exercise and a good diet together. However, there are certain amounts of exercise that you should meat in order to either lose the weight or maintain a healthy weight. Before you start you should remember that the way to lose one pound of fat is by consuming 3500 less calories in your diet. This means that if you want to lose a pound a week then you will need to burn at least 500 calories a day. You can cut either these calories out by eating less, exercising more, or doing a combination of both.

There are no magic exercise plans that work for everyone and help everyone to lose the weight. Each person has a different body and responds in different ways to certain types of exercise. It might take some trial and error in order to find out which exercises that you enjoy and which ones work the best for you.

If you are looking to exercise to lose weight there are some guidelines that you should follow. It is recommended by the Centers for Disease Control and Prevention that you try to get at least two hours and 30 minutes of exercise in a week in order to lose weight. This might sound like a lot but it ends up only being about 30 minutes five days a week; of course, the more exercise that you do, the greater the results of the weight loss. You will have to incorporate more exercise into your routine if you do not plan to cut back on your calories in order to see weight loss.

Some activities that you should include in your exercise plan include cardiovascular exercises such as walking, running, biking, hiking and swimming. In order to burn the largest amount of calories during your workout you need to elevate your heart rate and keep it at that rate for an extended time during the workout.

It is not a good idea to spend all of your time concentrating on aerobic exercises. While they are great for your heart and in helping you to burn calories and lose weight, you should include also other activities in your work out. These include strength training and stretching exercises, which can help make your bones and muscles stronger and help slim your waistline.

You can get just so many benefits from exercising. One of the benefits includes weight loss. Just for spending an hour doing a low impact exercise a 160 pound person can lose somewhere around 350 calories. If you decide to do a higher impact activity such as running you could lose up to 900 calories in that hour, which is way more than you need to burn in order to lose a pound per week.

Just how much exercise that you need in your exercise program will depend on how much weight you will want to lose? If you live a very sedentary life, and you want to lose a lot of weight, you will have to include more exercise in your day than someone who has a job that keeps them moving all day. It is a good idea to start with 30 minutes a couple of times a day and slowly build up to working out between 30-60 minutes at least five days a week.

Tips to Keep Motivated

Staying motivated on an exercise plan can be tough. You might start out with all of the best intentions, but after a few weeks or so, you will get worn out and not want to continue. It is much easier to just sit on the couch and hope that everything works out the way that you would like. While you know all of the great reasons to get up and do some exercising, it just is not as much fun, or at least is more work, than some of the other things you might want to do. Here are some of the best tips that you can use that will help you to keep motivated and get in a great workout every day.

Set some goals

Before you even head out to the gym, make sure that you are setting some goals. Make them challenging enough that you will need to put in some work, but simple enough that you would actually be able to get them done if you work hard. For example, it is not a good idea to say you will lose ten pounds a week, but saying you want to lose 2 pounds is reasonable.

Write down these goals from the beginning. They can be anything that you want as long as they give you a bit of a challenge and make you work for it. You can say that you will lose a certain amount of weight over time, go by the measurements in your body, or you can even choose to go for a specific amount of time or reps. It is up to you, just make sure that you are having some fun and working hard while at the gym.

Bring along music

Getting on the treadmill and staring at a wall for 30 to 60 minutes is going to get boring fast. You might enjoy it the first few times, but after that, the activity is not going to be as much fun and you will find that your motivation starts to slip away. This is why you should consider bringing something along to do while you are working out. This can be almost anything. Many people like to bring along some of their favorite music. This allows them to have something fun and upbeat to listen to while they are working out plus can get them pumped up and in the right mood to keep going.

Do an activity you love

It honestly does not matter how much you think an activity is going to help you to lose weight, if you are not enjoying it, you are less likely to keep up with it and you are not going to lose weight. Find something that you like doing, such as biking, swimming, weight lifting, walking, running, or maybe even a group class, and then do that. Even if it is not burning as many calories as another activity, at least you are having fun. The more fun you have with an activity, the better results you will have because you are more likely to keep going with it.

Try a new activity

It is always good to mix things up when you are at the gym. Even if you love an activity, you might find that after a few months of doing it all of the time, you are getting bored with it. Plus, your body is going to become used to a certain activity and you will not get the same results if you keep doing it. Find a few activities that you enjoy, or try a few new ones, and the switch them around on occasion. This allows you to do something new, continue having fun, and you can continue seeing results all at the same time.

Find a friend

For some people, the way that they get some motivation is to find a friend who is going to work out with them. This person should be someone who is looking for the same goals and who will be able to hold you accountable to show up. When you are doing the work outs on your own, it is easy to say that you'll get to it tomorrow and then you never go back. On the other hand, when you know that someone is waiting at the gym for you, you might feel a bit more obligated to show up. Once there, you might as well get in a good work out since you went to all of the trouble. This means you get in a work out much more often than you would on your own, and the results will be much better.

Get outside

You do not need to spend all of your time inside in the gym. When the weather is nice and you are having some trouble getting to the gym, why not take a good walk outside. This is one of the best ways to get in a good workout and can help to lift up your mood because you are getting plenty of fresh air and sunlight.

Reward yourself

Whenever you are able to reach some of your goals while working out, you should take the time to reward yourself. This allows you to feel good about the hard work you are doing and even gives you something to look forward to. You should not let the award be about food since you are trying to lose weight and this can ruin your plans. But choosing to go out a night with friends, go see a movie, purchase some new clothes, or give yourself a spa day can be great incentives to keep yourself going.

Each person is going to have some of their own methods to use that will motivate them to see success. While it might be hard to get on a good workout program, it is important to find a way to get on one and stick with it for your overall health. Once you get started and do it well for a few weeks, it becomes a routine and is much easier to do. Follow some of the tips in this chapter and see how easy it can be to get in your required work out each day.

The Benefits of Exercising

You have probably heard about it for your whole life. People have been telling you that exercise is important and that you should make sure to get in enough each and every day. But why is it so important to work out? Why can't you just sit on the couch and watch your favorite show instead of hitting the gym and trying to do all of that work. This chapter is going to spend a bit of time discussing the benefits that can come with exercising and why you need to get some in everyday.

Weight Loss

The first reason why many people will choose to exercise and work out is because they are looking to lose weight. Every weight loss and diet plan in the world will spell out how important it is to get in a good exercise program if you really want to lose weight. While limiting your calories can help out a lot, you are only able to limit those so much and exercising can help pick up the slack so that you are able to lose more. Pick a moderate to high intensity work out for the best results.

Heart Health

For you to really get a good workout, you will need to get that heart pumping and working hard. When the heart is functioning at this level, it is becoming stronger than ever before. When you sit on the couch, the heart barely has to move in order to get the nutrients all around the body so it is not becoming very strong. With a good work out that makes you sweat and gets the heart up a bit, you can work on its strength and become stronger in no time.

Brain Functioning

Studies have shown that getting in some exercise during the week is critical if you want your brain to function the way that it is supposed to. Exercise can help increase the flow of oxygen and blood to the brain which opens it up for working so much more efficiently. An added bonus is that exercise can help you out with your memory. This is important for those who are aging and need a bit of help recalling important events and facts. Of course, you may be able to find a lot of benefits of this as a younger person as well when you exercise right before a test and are better able to recall the facts you learn.

Stress

Stress is a daily part of life for most people and there is not much that they can do in order to get it to go away. But there are some things that you can do to reduce the amount of stress that you are feeling and to get yourself to look and feel better about the stress. Any time that the stress is starting to get too much for you, go and do a quick run or pop in your favorite work out movie. This will allow you to take a break from the stress you are feeling and you can better get back on track with other things.

Cholesterol

High cholesterol is a huge problem that a lot of people are dealing with because of the high fat diet found in this country. When you get on a good workout program, you can help to reduce the amount of bad cholesterol that is in the blood while also increasing the kind of good that is there.

Blood Pressure

When eating a diet that is high in sodium, or when you sit on the couch all day and do not perform some kind of physical activity, it is easy for you to get high blood pressure. One of the first things that the doctor is going to recommend that you do is get out and start exercising at least five days a week. This will allow the heart to function properly, your cholesterol to go lower, and your body to be better able to reduce the salts that are in there. All of this combines to allow your blood pressure to go way down.

Diabetes

Even the symptoms of diabetes can be controlled better when you are on a good exercise program. You will find that the body is able to metabolize the sugars that you are consuming much better when you are on this kind of program. Plus you are less likely to crave unhealthy and sugary foods so your insulin will not be under as much stress. If you are suffering from diabetes or pre-diabetes, it is best if you are able to get on a good workout program as soon as possible.

Mood

Your mood can be influenced by how much you exercise. Those who are depressed and down a lot of the time are the ones who rarely if ever get out there and do a good work out. Think about it this way, the few times that you have been to the gym and got in a really good workout how did you feel? Most people will say they felt good and that they were happy and on a little cloud for the rest of the day. Well, if you get on a good exercise program, you will be able to feel this way all of the time. Overall your mood will begin to improve. If you have depression, you may be able to cure it with a good exercise program. Even if you are not suffering from a mood disorder, you can benefit from the mood enhancement that comes from a good work out program.

Digestion

For many of those who are suffering from issues with their digestive tracts, a good work out program is able to help out with this. You should get in at least five days of moderate activity for 30 minutes on each day in order to see some of these great benefits on your digestive system in no time.

Self-confidence

For many, the way that they look and feel can determine how confident they are in themselves. When they start out on an exercise program and begin to lose weight, plus get all of the great health benefits that are listed above, they are going to feel a little bit better and you will notice a huge surge in the amount of self-confidence that they are feeling. They will begin to like the way that they look and will want to show it off. Just a few minutes of exercise each day can make this into a reality.

Conclusion

If you are trying to add more plants into your omnivorous or pescatarian diet or are trying to consider a more nutrient-dense palette of plants in a vegetarian or vegan diet, try to incorporate more whole foods and raw products, which have not been denatured due to heat and temperature. Here are some ways to start:

- Blend more vegetables together into soups, stews, and curries or adding them with fruit for a healthy breakfast smoothie or snack.

- Add 1-2 more vegetables into your sandwiches, stir-fries, and pasta dishes or make a garden salad as a side for your main meals.

- Opt for fresh fruit with nut butter such as almond or peanut butter that provides the complete number of macronutrients as a snack on the go throughout the day as an energy boost.

- Reach for a cold-pressed fruit and/or vegetable fruit juice with at least 3 different ingredients instead of a cup of java or caffeine

- Add more vegetables to your breakfast first thing in the morning such as spinach, tomatoes, and mushrooms to an omelets or scramble will help you easily get more plants earlier on in the day.

It is important to note that high cooking temperatures and over-processing of many vegetables and fruit can denature and remove the health benefits of their nutrient profile. Once a week, try a raw diet where you incorporate at least one meal or juice with all raw vegetables and fruit. Spiralized salads, fresh vegetable sticks, fresh fruit salads, and cold-pressed juices can allow you to incorporate more fruit and vegetables without sacrificing textures, flavors, vitamins, and minerals. Be aware that not all vegetables can be consumed raw: those that contain starches such as potatoes, most squash varieties, sweet potato, and taro cannot be consumed raw as the gut cannot breakdown the heavy starches. Many leafy greens can be consumed raw such as spinach, kale, and arugula but others like swiss chard, mustard greens, and broccolini may taste less bitter if they were fried or boiled. Be aware that the volume of vegetables also decreases when boiled, so it may appear that you may need to consume more cooked veggies to feel fuller. Most legumes are highly undigestible without cooking them down. However, you can choose to sprout many legume seeds such as sunflower seeds, mung beans, radish seeds, and broccoli seeds. These can be used to garnish salads and soups with plenty of health benefits and anti-inflammatory properties. If you are ever craving animal products, seek out these healthy, plant-based alternatives:

- Nutritional yeast instead of parmesan cheese
- Coconut bacon instead of pork bacon
- Extra firm tofu instead of chicken breasts
- Roasted cauliflower instead of chicken wings
- Cashew sauce instead of cream cheese
- Coconut whip instead of whipped cream
- Portobello mushroom caps instead of beef steak

Nutritional yeast is nutty in texture but does not contain any dairy by-products. It is also not a traditional yeast product used in baking or in brewing beer as it is intended to be consumed as a food product. Look for fortified nutritional yeast whereby vitamins are added to the manufacturing process. One tablespoon of nutritional yeast contains all nine essential amino acids as a complete protein that is required for human consumption. It also contains many B vitamins and minerals such as selenium, zinc, and manganese. Nutritional yeast is very beneficial to gut health, fighting off inflammation in the intestines, and removing toxins from certain food products.

Coconut bacon does not contain any meat by-product but is a crunchy alternative to the heavily processed and fatty pork bacon. It is made by drying out pieces of coconut flesh. It still contains a high fiber and protein profile but also contains polyunsaturated and monosaturated fats that help to increase HDL good cholesterol, unlike pork bacon which contains lots of saturated fat and may enhance LDL bad cholesterol.

Extra-firm tofu can handle high cooking temperatures or can be consumed raw after fermentation. It can be crumbled or cut into steaks and offers a chewy texture with a high protein profile, comparable to chicken breasts. It is also neutral in flavor and can absorb moisture and different seasonings and liquids to enhance its taste profile.

Cauliflower has been used commonly to replace chicken wings on restaurant menus. The texture of cauliflower when roasted, is slightly nutty and very crunchy on the outsides, while the insides tend to be soft and chewy like chicken wings. Cauliflower has a very nutrient-dense profile with a large amount of protein, fiber, Vitamin C, and Vitamin K which is helpful in blood circulation and supporting the immune system. Because it is so neutral in flavor, it can take on many sauces, flavorings, and seasonings – you can use your favorite seasonings for chicken wings as you would for cauliflower!

Cashew sauce is surprisingly very creamy in consistency due to its high content in healthy fats. Using a ratio volume of 1:3, cashews to water, you can soak the cashews overnight and blend them together to create this versatile, dairy-free sauce without any additives or stabilizers! It can be used for both desserts and savory dishes and can be stored in the fridge for a few weeks. You can add anything from paprika, curry powder, cumin, turmeric, or chilli powder to flavor this sauce! Coconut whip is made from coconut milk, blended on high for a few minutes in order to allow the liquid consistency to thicken. You can choose to sweeten the coconut whip with maple syrup and nutmeg. It has a very creamy texture without sacrificing any of its health benefits such as providing Vitamin E and fiber. It can be added to fruit snacks and desserts, in place of artificial whipped cream that is high in trans-fat. Portobello Mushrooms are very flavorful with an earthy, umami profile, that is like meat without any animal by-products. It is dense with the ability to hold a lot of different flavorings, sauces, and seasonings that you add to it. You can bake it, stir fry it, or boil it in soups and it will add a rich texture. It has many different minerals such as selenium, copper, and B vitamins, providing many anti-inflammatory benefits.

Plant-Based High-Protein Cookbook

A Complete Vegan Cookbook With Quick and Easy High-Protein Recipes For Bodybuilders

By

Joshua King

Introduction

What does it mean to be an athlete, bodybuilder, or any other sports professional? It's about making your active lifestyle the center of your career. It's about pushing yourself further and harder. It's about redefining your limits. To sum it up, your success depends on how you cook, what you eat, how you train, and everything in between. It realizes that who you are is defined by what you do. Athletes have the same number of hours in a day as everyone else.

However, that isn't enough. They need to make the most of every minute to stay on top of the game. You need to make time to eat three meals a day and fit in pre-workout and post-workout snacks. You need to work out to keep in shape and manage your weight. There are hours of training involved. Some games will lead up to competitions, tournaments, and championships.

You'll need time for your muscles to recover. Most importantly, you'll need a good night's sleep. These are essential to overall health as well as wellness.

How does a fitness enthusiast juggle it all? You'll need self-discipline. You'll need to work hard. But what does that have to do with the diet?

There is a saying that goes, "You are what you eat." That means that proper nutrition is crucial to be a good athlete. Which foods make for the strongest and healthiest individuals? Plant-based diets can provide a sports professional with all the protein, carbohydrates, and monosaturated fats they need to reach their full potential. That is because fruits and vegetables, legumes, nuts, and seeds are rich in nutrients, vitamins, minerals, and amino acids. More and more athletes are embracing veganism and are leading their best lives. That is because, after eating protein that comes from plants, sports professionals say they feel more energized and healthier emotionally, physically, and mentally. We'll read up more on that later.

This book does more than promote a vegan lifestyle. It will also guide you in making healthier food choices. The plant-based recipes featured here are high in protein. They taste great and will keep you feeling full. In addition to this, you will learn why it is essential to eat three meals a day and when is the best time to eat them. The recipes also provide background information on some of its' main ingredients. This is because it is good to know what we are putting into our bodies. We hope that with this additional information, you'll be confident that a plant-based diet will ensure optimal functionality for your body and brain.

Dieters and people trying to lose weight are not the only ones who get hit by a new type dieting that comes each year. With so many suggestions like low-fat, low-carb, gluten-free, etc., you just can't decide if you need to focus only on protein or on a whole new diet plan.

I understand your problem; I was in your shoes once. Since I was always changing my diet, lasting results were hard to get. I was going months before I could see new muscles building up. The problem was that my body got confused and didn't know how to configure itself to take the essential nutrients and proteins it needed to stay healthy and still build muscles.

Chapter 1. The Basic Of Plant-Based Diet

A plant-based diet is widely known for its obvious health advantages, and it has been tried and tested by people from all walks of life. Since it is a meat and dairy-free diet, there are those who assume it to be a low-protein diet—and that's where most of us are wrong. A plant-based diet can be a high-protein diet when consumed with the right approach and understanding. Such awareness is important for people building their muscles or who are involved in athletic activities, as they are the ones who need protein the most for the strengthening of their muscles. In this cookbook, we shall not only discuss the plant-based diet, but it is written with the purpose of providing a high-protein diet to the vegan bodybuilders and athletes. There are several plant-based sources that can be coupled with some plant-based supplements to meet the daily protein needs of a person.

To start with, let's get a clear view of the plant-based diet. This diet, though widely popular, is often confused with a vegetarian diet. The concept is to avoid all animal-sourced food products and rely completely on plant produce. The reasons can vary for each individual. Some may opt for a plant-based diet for its health benefits; others may want to adopt it to save animals—while few others may do so for both such reasons.

What constitutes a plant-based diet? By plant-sourced food, we mean all variety of vegetables, fruits, grains, legumes, lentils, plant oils, seeds, nuts, plant-based milk, grain flours, and vegan cheeses and milk. These products—or the food Prepared purely from them—is referred to as vegan or plant-based. In this list, we find that not a single ingredient is purely protein-based. While protein is largely present in most of the plant-sourced products, it is coupled with other macro and micronutrients as well. For athletes and bodybuilders, the concern is how to consume such products while balancing the proportion of these nutrients in the interest of their muscle building. And that concern leads us to the plant-based, vegan bodybuilding diet.

Chapter 2. What Vegan Is All About

A lot of people are doing it; a lot of individuals are talking about it, however, there is still a lot of confusion about what a whole food plant-based diet plan implies. Since we break food into its macronutrients: fats, proteins, and carbohydrates; many of us get confused about how to eat.

Whole foods are unprocessed foods that come from the earth. Now, we do consume some minimally processed foods on a whole foods plant-based diet such as entire bread, whole wheat pasta, tofu, non-dairy milk, and some nuts and seed butter the various categories: Whole grains Legumes (generally lentils and beans).

Fruits and veggies Nuts and seeds (including nut butter) Herbs and spices All the above-mentioned classifications make up the entire food plant-based diet. As long as you are eating foods like these regularly, you can forget about carbs, protein, and fat permanently.

Well, the appeal of a whole food plant-based diet plan is that if you don't like a particular food, like in this case, soy, then you do not have to consume it. It is not an essential element in an entire food plant-based diet instead of oats, quinoa instead of wheat; I'm sure you catch the drift now. It does not matter. Simply discover something that fits you.

Even if you have decided to embrace a plant-based diet plan way of life, it does not indicate that is a healthy diet plan. Plant-based diets have their fair share of scrap and other unhealthy eats; case and point, routine intake of vegetable pizzas and non-dairy ice cream. Staying healthy requires you to eat healthy foods-- even within a plant-based diet plan setting.

What to Look Out For When Adopting this Lifestyle

For a lot of people seeking to go plant-based, protein is always a significant concern. There is this idea that's perpetuated by the mainstream media backed by huge meat manufacturers that protein is just found in meat. Well, that's just not true. Standard staples such as nuts, beans, oats, and wild rice included a great deal of protein.

The fact is that foods like kale, broccoli, and almonds include lots of calcium. It's certainly from the greens they eat.

The major issue for a lot of plant-based diet plan followers is typically vitamin B12. B12, for everyone, is normally found in strengthened products, particularly cereals and plant-based milk.

You can adopt a healthy plant-based way of life by basing your diet around Prepared and raw foods filled with leafy and colorful veggies. These will provide your body with the minerals, vitamins, and antioxidants it requires.

Chapter 3.   Principles Of Bodybuilding Diet

Bodybuilding is categorized into three components. Within those three, are detailed steps into acquiring success into a phenomenal physique.

Step 1 : Diet & Nutrition

Bodybuilding is 80% diet and 20% lifting weights. Yes, it's true. What you take in, will result in the outcome of your physical well-being. There are a lot of myths and advertisements that emphasize protein drinks, creatine, pre-work out, etc,. Truth is, none of them are necessary in acquiring muscle and mass. They definitely do help, but like I explained they are not necessary. You can get all your energy, recovery, and mass from the right types of food. In fact, all those supplements that the majority of bodybuilders intake is actually harming your body.

Carbohydrates

Carbohydrates is an important nutrition that creates energy. They are split into three main categories: sugars, starches, and fiber. Most of the carbs in your diet into glucose, which provides energy. They are also turned into fats, which are saved till later use. Eating carbs in the morning will give you the energy to take on the day, and give you strength when training. The goal is to keep a balance in the intake of carbs. Distinguishing between good and bad carbs are vital to your energy and growing muscle.

Vitamins

Vitamins are also very important in bodybuilding and simply taking care of your health. From forming healthy teeth and bones, to maintaining brain function, there are many types of vitamins that help with bodybuilding and recovery.

Calcium

Not only does it help with promoting strong bones and teeth, it is essential for energy metabolism.

Foods that contain Calcium are almonds, cheese, seeds, and yogurts.

Biotin

Turns carbohydrates, protein, and fats into energy.

Foods that contain Biotin are peanut butter, eggs, almonds, and oats.

Iron

Iron transforms the oxygen from your lungs to your muscles and is vital to maintaining energy levels at its highest

Foods that contain Iron are bran cereals, beans, sardines, tofu, spinach, and whole wheat bread.

Vitamin C

Helps turn carbs into fuel and energy.

Foods that contain Vitamin C are broccoli, green and red peppers, brussels sprouts, cauliflower, and spinach.

Vitamin D

Helps absorb calcium, which is essential for muscle contractions.

Foods that contain Vitamin D are eggs, meat, milk, salmon, and fish such as sardines.

Vitamin B12

Vitamin B12 helps form red blood cells, and converts food into energy. It also helps the brain and muscles to communicate effectively resulting in coordination and muscle growth.

Foods that contain Vitamin B12 are eggs, meat, milk, and cheese.

Copper

Copper helps strengthen the tendon tendons needed to lift weights.

Foods that contain Copper are peanuts, crabs and lobsters, seeds, and dark chocolate.

Protein

Protein should be about half of your diet program. It helps oxygen flow through your body as well as building and repairing muscle tissues. Protein, when combined with intense training, help people add muscle mass or simply maintain. They are essentially used to recover from a work-out. Protein powders are popular amongst the bodybuilding crowd as it is easily accessible and helps grow muscles.

These three nutrition, when combined with your weightlifting, will bring significant results. As your body has all of the attributes that these foods and diets have, it is necessary to take in foods that are rich in carbohydrates, vitamins, and protein. Especially, protein. You can obtain all the right essential needs for a great bodybuilding diet from these foods listed above.

Step 2 : Training Plan

Now there are a lot of ways to approach your training plan. An important tool to get you going and to keep you consistent is to create a plan. Schedule a time when you will go to the gym and for how long. Setting a plan and goal daily will keep you to become consistent. Determine how many days a week you will take a rest, as rest is essential to growth. Then, create a plan in which muscle groups you will focus on Day 1, Day 2, and Day 3, so on and so forth. For example, as soon as I wake up, I eat breakfast and head straight to the gym. I then, determine which muscle group I am going to focus on and head straight towards the machine/equipment that are free weights. Free weights are weights such as the bench press, dumb bells, and barbells.

The best way to approach a work out is to start off with free weights. The free weights should work out the muscle group you are focusing on in the biggest and hardest way possible. One warm-up set should be plenty. After about 5-10 sets, go to another free weight for another 5 sets, give or take a few. After about 10 - 15 sets of free weights, go to a machine with a cable that will give your muscle group resistance. After about 2 exercises for about 5 -7 sets each, work on another exercise that will work out the small muscle groups within that muscle groups.

The repetition in each set should be according to the amount of weight you are lifting. When starting off for the first time, or getting back to training from a long break, it is important to form the core of the muscle group first. Start off with low weights, about 60% of what you could actually lift. The repetition goal should be 20 reps and up. Remember, this is just building the core of the muscle, when you are just starting off. This will bring significant results in the first month of your training, maybe less. Sam, a person I was training used this method and he was shocked at how much he improved in a month. He was able to bench press one plate, equal to 135 lbs for about 6-7 reps. Using this method, he put on 25lbs on each side equivalent to 95lbs, and did 20 reps each set for a week and a half. At the end of the week and a half, he was able to hit 30 reps non-stop. He then moved up to 35lbs on each side in the 2nd week equaling in 115bs. He did this for 2 weeks. After the 1st month was done, his bench press improved drastically. He was about to lift 165lbs, on the bench press machine for 2-3 reps. He was able to lift one plate(135lbs.) 10-12 reps easily.

It is not the amount of weight you can lift but the form and consistent improvement. In 2 months after following this method, Sam upped his weights and now went into the regular weight and regular repetition amount. The regular amount should be the weight able to lift in a repetition of 6-8. Even 10 repetition would be good. In the 6th month of training, Sam was now lifting heavily in an average repetition of 6. I have trained him for a year. Within that year, the diet plan, training plan, and rest plan I provided him with brought staggering results.

This method of training is the most basic type of bodybuilding. As you further your improvement in strength, knowledge, and endurance in your road to bodybuilding success, there are different ways you can approach your work out. Now the most important part of bodybuilding is rest.

Step 3 : Rest

Taking on the right approach to your diet, and putting in consistent levels of weight training, your body needs to replenish and refuel. This is when rest comes in. Growth comes from rest. Your body gains muscle, strength, and mass, in the period of sleeping and resting. When my father was training for his bodybuilding competitions, he would work out twice a day for a total of 5 hours. In between his work outs he would take power naps. Naps consisting of about 20 - 40 minutes of sleep. Society today are embedded with the concept of working hard and taking no days off. This will bring you above average results. Your goal is to work smarter, and bring exceptional results. 2 days a week of rest and 5 days of training is a good method. However, the method that I use brought me results that will change a person's physique significantly. For 10 days in a row, I work out every single day, and in those 10 days 4-5 I will go twice. Once in the morning and once in the evening. Your goal is to work out to the point where your muscle group will be almost torn. Vigorously working out, with high intensity training, and then for the next 2 -3 days I would rest. This will allow your muscles to grow exponentially and give you time to refuel. Afterwards, repeat the method. Your goal is to work out to the point where your muscles feel like it is almost tearing, and then rest. The number of days can be altered varying on the person's schedule, but this is how I do it, and it worked wonderfully for me. I like to add some cardio, such as running, or swimming throughout the 10 days to keep my stamina and endurance balanced.

Bodybuilding is a long term commitment of consistency and how much a person is willing to put in. The more you put in, the better your results will be. Bodybuilding helps you mentally, and it is a path that can you bring you success, not only in your physical state, but your work and your personal growth.

Chapter 4. Muscle Gains & Veganism

Every bodybuilder, irrespective of gender, strives to build a strong musculature through heavy training and intensive resistance exercises. And mere exercises can't make much of a difference when there isn't a good diet to support the body changes. Nutrients play a major role in muscle development, and the role of both the macro and the micronutrients cannot be overlooked. Experts believe that for optimal muscle development, about 0.7–1 gram of protein per pound of body weight per day is essential to consume. Keep these values in mind while we make a case for our high protein vegan diet. A bodybuilder must also have a 20% surplus of caloric intake for building and strengthening muscles.

The rise of the plant-based diet has also attracted many athletes and bodybuilders, but many have been skeptical and hesitant to opt for this approach as they were not aware of how a plant-based diet can also be a good source of protein and calories.

This particular concern of bodybuilders led many health experts and nutritionists to work extensively on the vegan diet and create high-protein recipes and develop a dietary approach which can specifically meet the needs of the people who are working for muscle gain. Where most people can simply rely on vegetables, fruits, grains, etc., to meet their energy needs, athletes should look into the diet very carefully and manage the high-protein to carb ratio while maintaining the intake of micronutrients and trace minerals. In a nutshell, a vegan bodybuilding diet is entirely different from a basic plant-based diet, as it is targeted to meet the need of building muscles.

Potential Benefits of the Vegan Bodybuilding Diet

Besides high-protein plant-based alternatives, this diet can provide several other health benefits to a bodybuilder. Let see how this diet can beat the negative effects of a non-vegan dietary approach and how well it can turn out to be for all those who are struggling to gain physical fitness.

Reduces heart disease risk

People consuming animal meat and fats are at more risk of developing heart diseases. The problem basically starts with bad cholesterol, also known as low-density lipoproteins. LDL is largely present in animal or saturated fats and it has the tendency to deposit into the blood vessels. The LDL is present in some amount in all the animal products from meat to dairy. A diet rich in those products can increase the LDL intake which consequently causes heart problems due to obstruction of blood vessels.

The vegan diet provides alternative cholesterol known as high-density lipoproteins, the good cholesterol which can bind the LDL with itself and removes it out of the blood. It does not deposit into the blood vessels and prevents several heart diseases.

Can promote a healthy body weight

For bodybuilders and athletes, there is a constant strive for an ideal or healthy body weight. When the vegan diet is compared to any traditional diet, the results clearly show how well it helps in maintaining body mass index. The plant-based diet does not add up to the body fats. For zero-fat body weight, the vegan diet seems idea for the physical fitness of every person involved in athletic activities. Since it can maintain body weight, it also keeps the problems of insulin resistance and low metabolic activities away from the person.

Protects against certain cancers

Nearly everyone vulnerable to cancer, or the ones suffering from the early stages of it, are prescribed the plant-based diet. There are many features of this diet that can prevent or treat the negative effects of cancer. Firstly, the plants with their phytonutrients have a therapeutic tendency and heal the cellular mutation that can cause cancer. Moreover, this diet makes the body resistant and strong towards the deleterious effects of cancer.

Chapter 5. Plant Based Diet For Health

Dr. David C Nieman, the director of the Human Performance Laboratory at Appalachia State University in North Carolina, has studied the effects of diet on athletes and their fitness. His subject of study focused on physical fitness and its association with a plant-based or vegan diet.

Dr. Nieman is himself a marathon runner and happens to be a vegetarian. It was his personal interest to learn more about the effects of a vegan diet. According to him, the vegan diet can only prove healthy for the people who are involved in extreme physical exercises and remain engaged in such activities for more than an hour. He suggests a high-protein, low-carb vegan diet to control carb intake. In this way, a person can gain more muscle endurance and improvement in overall body shape and size.

There are also other studies that correlate the vegan diet and physical performance of a person. However, the work in this area is limited so far. However, there are many examples to look up to for inspiration. There are plenty of bodybuilders out there who are vegan and still manage to maintain an ideal body mass index, excellent muscle shape, and a great size.

Torre Washington is a good example. He has practically never tasted meat in his life but no one can guess that with the looks of his muscles and body shape. He was raised in a vegetarian family and grew up eating all kinds of plant-based food. Today he is a certified coach at the National Academy of Sports Medicine and a professional bodybuilder and a sprinter. He switched to veganism about twenty years ago, and he has become a vegan bodybuilding champion though his tailored vegan diet. Torre is a living example of how a vegan diet can best support muscle growth.

Nimai Delgado is another example that comes to mind when we discuss veganism and bodybuilding. Nimai has won the Fresno classic USA championships, Sacramento Pro, Hawaii Pro, and Grand Prix due to his well-maintained physique.

He is now a professional bodybuilder and athlete. He was also a vegetarian from early childhood, and later switched to a 95% vegan diet back in 2015. His muscle shape and size are good enough to give a befitting response to all the critics of the vegan bodybuilding diet.

Patrik Baboumian, an Armenian-German athlete, has also proved the power of plant protein through his great shape and rock-solid muscles. Patrik has been using a vegan diet for the last five years of his twenty-three-year career. And today he feels stronger than ever before. He is quite vocal about the benefits of a vegan diet for bodybuilding and he also uses his social media accounts to debunk all the myths around veganism.

Chapter 6.   High Protein Daily Recipes

Stuffed Avocados

Preparation time: 15 minutes

Servings: 2

Ingredients

1 large avocado, halved and pitted

1 cup cooked chickpeas

¼ cup walnuts, chopped

¼ cup celery stalks, chopped

1 scallion (green part), sliced

1 small garlic clove, minced

1½ tablespoons fresh lemon juice

½ teaspoon olive oil

Salt and ground black pepper, to taste

1 tablespoon sunflower seeds

1 tablespoon fresh cilantro, chopped

How to Prepare

With a spoon, scoop out the flesh from each avocado half.

Then, cut half of the avocado flesh in equal-sized cubes.

In a large bowl, add avocado cubes and remaining ingredients except for sunflower seeds and cilantro and toss to coat well.

Stuff each avocado half with chickpeas mixture evenly.

Serve immediately with the garnishing of sunflower seeds and cilantro.

Nutrition Calories 440

Total Fat 32.2 g Saturated Fat 5 g

Cholesterol 0 mg   Sodium 428 mg

Total Carbs 30.2 g   Fiber 14.4 g

Sugar 2.3 g   Protein 12.6 g

Stuffed Sweet Potatoes

Preparation time: 20 minutes

Cooking time: 40 minutes

Total time: 1 hour

Servings: 2

Ingredients

Sweet Potatoes

1 large sweet potato, halved

½ tablespoon olive oil

Salt and ground black pepper, to taste

Filling

½ tablespoon olive oil

1/3 cup canned chickpeas, rinsed and drained

1 teaspoon curry powder

1/8 teaspoon garlic powder

1/3 cup cooked quinoa

Salt and ground black pepper, to taste

1 teaspoon fresh lime juice

1 teaspoon fresh cilantro, chopped

1 teaspoon sesame seeds

How to Prepare

Preheat the oven to 375°F.

Rub each sweet potato half with oil evenly.

Arrange the sweet potato halves onto a baking sheet, cut-side down, and sprinkle with salt and black pepper.

Bake for 40 minutes, or until sweet potato becomes tender.

Meanwhile, for filling: in a skillet, heat the oil over medium heat and cook the chickpeas, curry powder, and garlic powder for about 6–8 minutes, stirring frequently.

Stir in the cooked quinoa, salt, and black pepper, and remove from the heat.

Remove from the oven and arrange each sweet potato halves onto a plate.

With a fork, fluff the flesh of each half slightly.

Place chickpea mixture in each half and drizzle with lime juice

Serve immediately with the garnishing of cilantro and sesame seeds.

Nutrition

Calories 340

Total Fat 8.2 g

Saturated Fat 1.1 g

Cholesterol 0 mg

Sodium 117 mg

Total Carbs 50 g

Fiber 10 g

Sugar 8.8 g

Protein 12.6 g

Cauliflower with Peas

Preparation time: 15 minutes

Cooking time: 15 minutes

Servings: 3

Ingredients

2 medium tomatoes, chopped

¼ cup water

2 tablespoons olive oil

3 garlic cloves, minced

½ tablespoon fresh ginger, minced

1 teaspoon ground cumin

2 teaspoons ground coriander

1 teaspoon cayenne pepper

¼ teaspoon ground turmeric

2 cups cauliflower, chopped

1 cup fresh green peas, shelled

Salt and ground black pepper, to taste

½ cup warm water

How to Prepare

In a blender, add tomato and ¼ cup of water and pulse until a smooth puree forms. Set aside.

In a large skillet, heat the oil over medium heat and sauté the garlic, ginger, green chilies, and spices for about 1 minute.

Add the cauliflower, peas, and tomato puree and cook, stirring for about 3–4 minutes.

Add the warm water and bring to a boil.

Reduce the heat to medium-low and cook, covered for about 8–10 minutes or until vegetables are done completely. Serve hot.

Nutrition   Calories 163

Total Fat 10.1 g   Saturated Fat 1.5 g

Cholesterol 0 mg   Sodium 79 mg

Total Carbs 16.1 g   Fiber 5.6 g

Sugar 6.7 g   Protein 6 g

Burgers with Mushroom Sauce

Preparation time: 25 minutes

Cooking time: 30 minutes

Servings: 2

Ingredients

Patties

½ cup millet, rinsed

1 cup hot water

1 (14-ounce) can chickpeas, rinsed, drained, and mashed roughly

1 carrot, peeled and grated finely

½ of red bell pepper, seeded and chopped

½ of yellow onion, chopped

1 garlic clove, minced

½ tablespoon fresh cilantro, chopped

½ teaspoon curry powder

Salt and ground black pepper, to taste

4 tablespoons chickpea flour

2 tablespoons canola oil

Mushroom Sauce

2 cups unsweetened soymilk

2 tablespoons arrowroot flour

1 tablespoon low-sodium soy sauce

Pinch of ground black pepper

1 teaspoon olive oil

¾ cup fresh button mushrooms, chopped

1 garlic clove, minced

2 tablespoons fresh chives, chopped

How to Prepare

For patties: heat a small non-stick pan over medium heat and toast the millet for about 5 minutes, stirring continuously.

Add the hot water and bring to a rolling boil.

Reduce the heat to low and simmer, covered for about 15 minutes.

Remove from the heat and set aside, covered for about 10 minutes.

Uncover the pan and let the millet cool completely.

After cooling, fluff the millet with a fork.

In a large bowl, add the millet and remaining ingredients (except for chickpea flour and oil) and mix until well combined.

Slowly, add the chickpea flour, 1 tablespoon at a time, and mix well.

Make 4 equal-sized patties from the mixture.

In a non-stick frying pan, heat the oil over medium heat and cook the patties for about 3–4 minutes per side, or until golden-brown.

Meanwhile, for mushroom sauce: in a bowl, add the soymilk, flour, soy sauce, and black pepper and beat until smooth. Set aside.

Heat the oil in a skillet over medium heat and sauté the mushrooms and garlic for about 3 minutes. Stir in the soymilk mixture and cook for about 8 minutes, stirring frequently. Stir in the chives and remove from the heat. Place 2 patties onto each serving plate and top with mushroom sauce. Serve immediately.

Nutrition Calories 713 Total Fat 24.2 g Saturated Fat 2.3 g

Cholesterol 0 mg   Sodium 674 mg Total Carbs 92 g

Fiber 17.1 g Sugar 8.5 g   Protein 29.5 g

Rice & Lentil Loaf

Preparation time: 20 minutes

Cooking time: 1 hour 50 minutes

Total time: 2 hours 10 minutes

Servings: 6

Ingredients

1¾ cups plus 2 tablespoons water, divided

½ cup wild rice

½ cup brown lentils

Salt, to taste

½ teaspoon Italian seasoning

1 medium yellow onion, chopped

1 celery stalk, chopped

6 cremini mushrooms, chopped

4 garlic cloves, minced

¾ cup rolled oats

½ cup walnuts, chopped finely

¾ cup sugar-free ketchup

½ teaspoon red pepper flakes, crushed

1 teaspoon fresh rosemary, minced

2 teaspoons fresh thyme, minced

How to Prepare

In a pan, add 1¾ cups of the water, rice, lentils, salt, and Italian seasoning over medium-high heat and bring to a rolling boil.

Reduce the heat to low and cook, covered for about 45 minutes.

Remove the pan from heat and set aside, covered for at least 10 minutes.

Preheat your oven to 350°F and line a 9x5-inch loaf pan with parchment paper.

In a skillet, heat the remaining water over medium heat and sauté the onion, celery, mushrooms, and garlic for about 4–5 minutes.

Remove from the heat and set aside to cool slightly.

In a large bowl, add the oats, walnuts, ketchup, and fresh herbs and mix until well combined.

Add the rice mixture and vegetable mixture and mix well.

In a blender, add the mixture and pulse until just a chunky mixture forms.

Place the mixture into the Prepared loaf pan evenly.

With a piece of foil, cover the loaf pan and bake for about 40 minutes.

Uncover and bake for 20 minutes more, or until top becomes golden-brown.

Remove from the oven and place the loaf pan onto a wire rack for about 10 minutes.

Carefully, invert the loaf onto a platter.

Cut into desired sized slices and serve.

Nutrition

Calories 254 Total Fat 7.5 g Saturated Fat 0.6 g

Cholesterol 0 mg   Sodium 269 mg Total Carbs 38.6 g

Fiber 8.5 g Sugar 8.9 g   Protein 11.5 g

Chickpeas with Swiss Chard

Preparation time: 15 minutes

Cooking time: 15 minutes

Servings: 4

Ingredients

2 tablespoons olive oil

1 medium yellow onion, chopped

4 garlic cloves, minced

1 teaspoon dried thyme, crushed

1 teaspoon dried oregano, crushed

½ teaspoon paprika

1 cup tomato, chopped finely

2½ cups canned chickpeas, rinsed and drained

5 cups Swiss chard

2 tablespoons water

2 tablespoons fresh lemon juice

Salt and ground black pepper, to taste

3 tablespoons fresh basil, chopped

How to Prepare

Heat the olive oil in a skillet over medium heat and sauté onion for about 6-8 minutes.

Add the garlic, herbs, and paprika and sauté for about 1 minute.

Add the Swiss chard and 2 tablespoons water and cook for about 2-3 minutes.

Add the tomatoes and chickpeas and cook for about 2-3 minutes.

Add in the lemon juice, salt, and black pepper, and remove from the heat.

Serve hot with the garnishing of basil.

Nutrition

Calories 260 Total Fat 8.6 g Saturated Fat 1.1 g

Cholesterol 0 mg   Sodium 178 mg Total Carbs 34 g

Fiber 8.6 g Sugar 3.1 g   Protein 12 g

Spicy Black Beans

Preparation time: 15 minutes

Cooking time: 1 hour 25 minutes

Total time: 1 hour 40 minutes

Servings: 5

Ingredients

4 cups water

1½ cups dried black beans, soaked for 8 hours and drained

½ teaspoon ground turmeric

3 tablespoons olive oil

1 small red onion, chopped finely

1 green chili, chopped

1 (1-inch) piece fresh ginger, minced

2 garlic cloves, minced

1½ tablespoons ground coriander

1 teaspoon ground cumin

½ teaspoon cayenne pepper

Salt, to taste

2 medium tomatoes, chopped finely

¼ cup coconut cream

½ cup fresh cilantro, chopped

How to Prepare

In a large pan, add water, black beans, and turmeric, and bring to a boil on high heat.

Now, reduce the heat to low and cook, covered for about 1 hour or until desired doneness of beans. Meanwhile, in a skillet, heat the oil over medium heat and sauté the onion for about 4–5 minutes. Add the green chili, ginger, garlic, spices, and salt, and sauté for about 1–2 minutes. Stir in the tomatoes and cook for about 10 minutes, stirring occasionally. Transfer the tomato mixture into the pan with black beans and stir to combine. Reduce the heat to medium-low and cook for about 20–25 minutes. Serve hot with the garnishing of coconut cream and cilantro.

Nutrition   Calories 344   Total Fat 11.9 g   Saturated Fat 3.8 g

Cholesterol 0 mg   Sodium 50 mg   Total Carbs 48.5 g

Fiber 10 g   Sugar 10.8 g   Protein 13.6 g

Mixed Bean Soup

Preparation time: 20 minutes

Cooking time: 45 minutes

Total time: 1 hour 5 minutes

Servings: 12

Ingredients

¼ cup vegetable oil

1 large onion, chopped

1 large sweet potato, peeled and cubed

3 carrots, peeled and chopped

3 celery stalks, chopped

3 garlic cloves, minced

2 teaspoons dried thyme, crushed

1 (4-ounce) can green chilies

2 jalapeño peppers, chopped

1 tablespoon ground cumin

4 large tomatoes, chopped finely

2 (16-ounce) cans great northern beans, rinsed and drained

2 (15¼-ounce) cans red kidney beans, rinsed and drained

1 (15-ounce) can black beans, drained and rinsed

9 cups homemade vegetable broth

1 cup fresh cilantro, chopped

How to Prepare

In a Dutch oven, heat the oil over medium heat and sauté the onion, sweet potato, carrots, and celery for about 6–8 minutes.

Add the garlic, thyme, green chilies, jalapeño peppers, and cumin and sauté for about 1 minute.

Add in the tomatoes and cook for about 2–3 minutes. Add the beans and broth and bring to a boil over medium-high heat. Cover the pan with lid and cook for about 25–30 minutes. Stir in the cilantro and remove from heat. Serve hot.

Nutrition Calories 563

Total Fat 6.8 g Saturated Fat 1.4 g   Cholesterol 0 mg   Sodium 528 mg

Total Carbs 90 g   Fiber 31.5 g Sugar 11 g   Protein 32.4 g

Barley & Lentil Stew

Preparation time: 20 minutes

Cooking time: 50 minutes

Total time: 1 hour 10 minutes

Servings: 8

Ingredients

2 tablespoons olive oil

2 carrots, peeled and chopped

1 large red onion, chopped

2 celery stalks, chopped

2 garlic cloves, minced

1 teaspoon ground coriander

2 teaspoons ground cumin

1 teaspoon cayenne pepper

1 cup barley

1 cup red lentils

5 cups tomatoes, chopped finely

5–6 cups homemade vegetable broth

6 cups fresh spinach, torn

Salt and ground black pepper, to taste

How to Prepare

In a large pan, heat the oil over medium heat and sauté the carrots, onion, and celery for about 5 minutes.

Add the garlic and spices and sauté for about 1 minute.

Add the barley, lentils, tomatoes, and broth and bring to a rolling boil.

Reduce the heat to low and simmer, covered for about 40 minutes.

Stir in the spinach, salt, and black pepper, and simmer for about 3–4 minutes.

Serve hot.

Nutrition Calories 264

Total Fat 5.8 g Saturated Fat 1 g   Cholesterol 0 mg   Sodium 540 mg

Total Carbs 41.1 g   Fiber 14.1 g Sugar 5.8 g   Protein 14.3 g

Chapter 7.   Breakfast And Smoothie Recipes

Carrots and Raisins Muffin

Servings: 4

Preparation time: 5 minutes

Cooking time: 30 minutes

Ingredients

1 1/4 cup almond flour

1/2 cup whole grain flour (any)

3 Tbsp ground almonds

2 cups carrot, grated

1 1/2 tsp baking soda

2 tsp baking powder

2 tsp cinnamon

1/2 tsp salt

1 tsp apple vinegar

1/2 cup extra-virgin olive oil

2 Tbsp linseed oil

4 Tbsp organic honey

3 oz raisins seedless

Directions:

Preheat oven to 360 F.

In a big bowl, combine together almond flour, whole grain flour, baking soda, baking powder, cinnamon, and salt.

In a separate bowl, whisk apple vinegar, olive oil, linseed oil, and honey.

Combine almond flour mixture with liquid mixture; stir well.

Add in the shredded carrots and raisins; stir well.

Fill the muffin cups 3/4 of the way full.

Bake for 30 minutes.

Remove from the oven, and allow to cool for 10 minutes.

Serve.

Easy Vegan Tacos

Servings: 2

Preparation time: 5 minutes

Cooking time: 10 minutes

Ingredients:

Taco Shells (8)

Corn (.25 C.)

Chopped Cherry Tomatoes (8)

Chopped Avocado (1)

Ground Cumin (2 t.)

Hot Sauce (2 t.)

Tomato Puree (1 C.)

Black Beans (2 C.)

Directions: To begin this recipe, you will want to take a pan and place it over medium heat. As the pan begins to warm up, add in the tomato puree, black beans, hot sauce, and cumin. Cook all of these ingredients together for about five minutes or until everything is warmed through. At this point, feel free to season the dish however you would like.   Next, you will begin to assemble the tacos. All you need to do is pour in as much or as little bean mixture into each taco

Porridge with Oatmeal and Maca Powder

Servings: 2

Preparation time: 5 minutes

Cooking time: 10 minutes

Ingredients

2 cups almond milk (or coconut milk) unsweetened

1 pinch of table salt

1 cup rolled oats

1 1/2 Tbsp Maca powder

1 Tbsp honey (or maple syrup)

1 tsp ground cinnamon

1 banana peeled and thinly sliced

Directions: In a saucepan, heat almond milk with a pinch of salt over high heat; bring to boiling. Stir in rolled oats and Maca powder, reduce heat to medium and simmer, uncovered, for 5 to 7 minutes; stir constantly. Place oatmeal in a bowl and pour over the honey, cinnamon, and banana slices. Serve and enjoy!

Savory Potato-Turmeric Pancakes

Servings: 4

Preparation time: 5 minutes

Cooking time: 15 minutes

Ingredients

4 large potatoes, grated

1 tsp of turmeric powder

1 Tbsp almond butter with salt added

Salt and ground pepper to taste

1/2 cup of garlic-infused olive oil

Serving: fresh chopped parsley or sliced green onions

Directions: Peel, wash, and pat dry potatoes. Grate potatoes over a plate or bowl. Season potatoes with the salt and pepper and turmeric.

Heat oil in a large frying skillet over medium-strong heat Spoon grated potatoes into hot oil and press with a spatula. Cook for about 2 minutes; flip the pancake and cook until golden brown. Transfer pancake to the kitchen paper towel. Serve warm with chopped parsley or green onion.

Sheer Vegan Meatza

Servings: 3

Preparation time: 15 minutes

Cooking time: 50 minutes

Ingredients

Cauliflower Crust

1/2 cup avocado oil

1 head cauliflower cut into florets

1/2 tsp garlic minced

Salt and ground pepper to taste

1/2 cup button mushrooms thinly sliced

2 Tbsp arrowroot powder

Filling/topping

1/2 cup of ketchup

1 cup mushrooms sliced

1 cup avocado puree (mashed)

1/2 cup grated carrot

1 cup olives, pitted, sliced or halved

Directions:

Cauliflower dough:

Preheat oven to 400F.

Cover a baking sheet with parchment paper.

Add cauliflower florets into your food processor into batches.

Process cauliflower florets until they achieve a form of rice.

Cook cauliflower in non-stick frying skillet for about 8 to 10 minutes.

Transfer cauliflower rice into a bowl and add mushrooms, ground garlic, arrowroot powder, some oil, and the salt and pepper; stir well.

Spread cauliflower dough onto a prepared baking sheet, and bake for about 20 minutes.

Remove from oven, and allow it to cool for 10 minutes.   Toppings

Fill the dough with ketchup, avocado puree, sliced mushrooms, carrot, and sprinkle with little avocado oil.   Place dough in the oven and bake for 10 to 12 minutes. Slice and serve hot.

Sour Edamame Spread

Servings: 6

Preparation time: 5 minutes

Cooking time: 5 minutes

Ingredients

2 cups frozen unshelled edamame, cooked according to package directions

1/4 cup sesame oil , 1 cup silken tofu, drained

1 Tbsp minced garlic (from 3 medium cloves)

Flaky sea salt to taste

White pepper to taste

2 tsp ground cumin , 1 Tbsp rice vinegar, 4 Tbsp fresh lemon juice

Sesame seeds for serving

Directions: Place all ingredients into your high-speed blender or into a food processor. Blend until combined well. Transfer spread to a bowl and a sprinkle with sesame seeds. Edamame spread can be refrigerated in an airtight container up to 3 days.

Stamina Tofu "Omelette"

Servings: 2

Preparation time: 8 minutes

Cooking time: 12 minutes

Ingredients

2 Tbsp of olive oil

1 small onion finely chopped

1 large red pepper chopped

1/2 cup white mushrooms halved or sliced

3/4 lb tofu cut into cubes, 1 Tbsp nutritional yeast

1 tsp turmeric (for color), 1 tsp of garlic powder

Sea salt and ground black pepper to taste

Directions: Heat oil in a large frying pan over medium-high heat. Sauté onion and red pepper with a pinch of salt for 2 to 3 minutes. Add mushrooms and cook until most of the water from the mushrooms has evaporated. Add tofu cubes and all remaining ingredients; stir well. Cover and cook over medium heat for about 6 to 8 minutes; stir occasionally. Taste and adjust seasonings. Serve hot.

Superelan Vegan Quark Smoothie

Servings: 2

Preparation time: 5 minutes

Cooking time: 5 minutes

Ingredients

1 frozen banana

3/4 cup frozen berries

1 apple cored and sliced

1/3 cup oats

1 scoop vegan protein powder (Soy or Hemp Protein)

3/4 cup vegan quark (for example Alpro)

1 1/2 cups almond milk

Directions:

Place all ingredients into your fast-speed blender.

Blend until smooth and creamy.

Serve immediately.

Sweet Potato and Orange Breakfast Bread

Servings: 6

Preparation time: 5 minutes

Cooking time: 50 minutes

Ingredients

1 large sweet potato (about 12 oz.), peeled and shredded

1/2 cup fresh orange juice

1/3 cup water

1/3 cup orange marmalade

4 Tbsp canola oil

1 Tbsp arrowroot powder

3 cups flour self-rising

1/2 cup sugar

2 tsp baking powder

1/4 tsp salt

Directions:

Preheat oven to 375 F/180 C.

In a small saucepan, cook the shredded sweet potato for 10 min; drain and cool.

In a bowl, combine shredder potato with orange juice, water, orange marmalade, canola oil, and arrowroot powder.

In a separate bowl, combine together the flour, sugar, baking powder, and salt.

Add the liquid ingredients to the flour mixture and stir just until combined.

Spoon batter into greased loaf pan and bake for 30-35 minutes.

When ready, allow it to cool for 10 minutes.

Slice and serve.

The Power of Banana & Soya Smoothie

Servings: 2

Preparation time: 5 minutes

Cooking time: 5 minutes

Ingredients

3/4 cup soya milk

2 bananas frozen

1 kiwi fruit sliced

1 Tbsp hemp seeds

1 Tbsp linseed oil

1 scoop vegan protein powder (pea or soy protein)

1 cup fresh spinach

3/4 cup frozen berries thawed (unsweetened)

Directions:

Place all ingredients in your blender.

Blend for about 45 seconds or until everything is well mixed. Serve.

Vegan Parsley and Almond Bread

Servings: 2

Preparation time: 10 minutes

Cooking time: 1 hour

Ingredients

1 1/2 cups sparkling water on room temperature

1 Tbsp of active dry yeast

1 tsp sugar

3 Tbsp olive oil

2 1/2 cups self-rising flour

2 Tbsp fresh minced parsley

1/2 cup almonds finely chopped

1 tsp ground garlic

1 tsp salt

Directions:

Preheat oven to 375 F/185 C.

Grease a baking loaf with olive oil; set aside.

In a large bowl, dissolve yeast, sugar, and salt in sparkling water; let stand until bubbles form on the surface.

Add in flour and olive oil and beat until smooth.

Add all remaining ingredients, and continue to beat until combined well or until form soft dough.

Turn onto a floured surface; knead until smooth and elastic or for about 8 minutes.

Shape dough into a loaf, and place into a prepared bread loaf.

Bake for 30 to 35 minutes or until golden brown.

Remove from oven, and let sit for 10 minutes.

Slice, serve, and enjoy!

Vegan Sloppy Joe with Tofu

Servings: 4

Preparation time:

Cooking time:

Ingredients

2 Tbsp avocado oil

1 onion finely sliced

2 cloves garlic finely sliced

1 lb tofu cheese, cubed

1 jalapeno pepper sliced

1 green bell pepper, diced

1 large tomato diced

3 Tbsp tomato paste

2 Tbsp fajita spice mix

Salt and ground black pepper

1 cup of water

Directions:

Heat oil in large frying skillet over medium heat.

Add sliced green onion, garlic, green pepper, and jalapeno pepper; sauté with a pinch of pepper for 3 to 4 minutes or until soft.

Add tofu and brown for a further 3 minutes; stir constantly.

Add diced tomato, tomato paste, water, and fajita spice mix; cover and cook on medium-low heat for 10 minutes.

Taste and adjust salt and pepper to taste.

Serve immediately or keep refrigerated.

Vegan Super Green Giant Smoothie

Servings: 2

Preparation time: 5 minutes

Cooking time: 5 minutes

Ingredients

1 1/2 cups almond milk (or coconut milk)

1 cup of carrot tops chopped

1 cup fresh spinach chopped

1 cucumber, peeled and sliced

1 large banana, fresh or frozen

3 Tbsp ground almonds or ground Macadamia almonds

1 scoop vegan protein powder (pea or soy protein)

1 Tbsp extracted honey

1 Tbsp linseed oil

Directions: Place all ingredients in your fast-speed blender. Blend until smooth and combined well. Serve.

Vegan Sweet "French Toast"

Servings: 2

Preparation time: 5 minutes

Cooking time: 10 minutes

Ingredients

3 Tbsp olive oil

1 cup of soy milk (unsweetened)

1 cup oat flour (or buckwheat)

1/2 tsp cinnamon

2 Tbsp brown sugar or sugar

6 slices day-old bread (or multi-grain bread)

Servings; vegan spread, groundnuts, honey or Maple syrup

Directions:

Heat oil in a frying skillet over medium-high heat.

Pour soy milk in one bowl.

In a separate bowl, combine together oat flakes and brown sugar; stir well.

Dip each bread slice first in soy milk, and then roll into oat flakes mixture.

Fry your vegan French toast for a couple of minutes on each side, or until golden brown.

Remove French toast onto a lined plate with kitchen paper to drain.

Serve with your favorite vegan spread, groundnuts, honey or Maple syrup.

Spinach and Blueberry Protein Drink

Preparation time: 5 Minutes
Cooking time: None
Servings: 2

Ingredients:

½ cup of vegan yogurt

¼ cup of mixed berries

1/3 cup of non-dairy milk

1 cup of leafy greens

1 scoop of vegan protein powder

1/3 cup of ice

Directions:

Add all the ingredients into a food processor, except the ice

Blend until smooth, then add ice

Blend until ice is crushed, then serve

Pick Me Up Coffee Smoothie

Preparation Time: 5 Minutes
Cooking time: None
Servings: 2

Ingredients:

1 can coconut milk

3 frozen bananas

2 tbsp peanut butter

4 tsp instant coffee powder

2 tbsp maple syrup

Directions:

Peel and chop fresh bananas into pieces

Freeze for 2 hours before use

In a food processor, add non-dairy milk, frozen bananas, peanut butter, instant coffee powder and maple syrup

Blend until smooth

Strawberry Vegan Smoothie

Preparation Time: 5 Minutes
Cooking time: None
Servings: 2

Ingredients:

2 cups strawberries

1 banana

1/4 cup non-dairy milk

2 tbsp maple syrup

Directions:

In a food processor, blend strawberries, banana, milk and maple syrup

Pour in two serving glasses and enjoy

Avocado Green Smoothie

Preparation Time: 5 Minutes
Cooking time: None
Servings: 2

Ingredients:

1/2 avocado

1 banana

1 cup spinach

1 cup non-dairy milk

2 pitted dates

Directions:

In a food processor, blend the avocado, banana, spinach, milk and dates until smooth

Pour in two serving glasses and enjoy

Granola Bars

For some additional ideas of pre-workout snacks, consider a granola bar. What is it? The basic recipe contains oats, nuts and seeds and dried fruit. Oats, have fiber. It lowers cholesterol levels and reduces the risk of developing heart diseases.

The ingredients are then held together with maple syrup or agave. They are convenient because they are small and don't need to be kept cold. Since they often come pre-portioned, it prevents over-eating.

This makes it easier to manage weight. Granola bars also taste good and come in a variety of flavors. In terms of health benefits, granola bars can be a good source of fiber and protein, as well. However, just like with protein smoothies, not every granola bar is considered healthy. This is the case when it contains ingredients that can minimize the results of your training efforts.

Yes, granola bars can be a healthy choice for athletes. However, this isn't always the case. We recommend you check the ingredient list of those you buy at the grocery store. That's because artificial ingredients, high levels of sugar and added calories can impede on your fitness goals. They are often highly processed, which may be the cause of developing metabolic syndrome. It is responsible for several health conditions like diabetes, heart disease and a stroke.

Processed foods contain artificial ingredients, which means a consumer can't know with certainty what exactly they are ingesting. In addition to this, some store-bought granola bar brands go over the recommended amount of sugar you should eat in a day. Excess sugar is often the underlying cause of weight gain. If not controlled, this can lead to obesity and diabetes. Some people assume that sugar alcohols are better alternatives to sugar but have their share of problems. For instance, they may not be broken down by your body as effectively.

They may also present adverse effects to those with a sensitivity towards xylitol or sorbitol. Other artificial sweeteners like aspartame, saccharin and sucralose react negatively on one's gut health and make it more difficult for your body to keep blood sugar under control.

Knowing this, you are perhaps asking yourself what you should look for in a granola bar. For it to be healthy, it should be made up of real ingredients. These include grains such as oats, as well as fruit, seed and nuts. Ideally, real foods have ingredients that you can pronounce. Their sugar content should be under 10 grams. For it to be nourishing, it should have over 5 grams of protein. A healthy granola bar should also have a source of fiber, so at least 3 grams. As for the number of calories, it shouldn't exceed 250.

Furthermore, you should know that first impressions matter, when it comes to food. What do we mean by this? Simply put, ingredients are listed in the order they appear in. What the product has the most of will be listed first. Adversely, what the product has least of will be listed last. If sugar features among the granola bar's first three ingredients, then it should be avoided. It is not a healthy snack choice for you.

As a vegan, you must also check the ingredient list to be sure it is 100% plant-based. Because of the hassle, it can be to choose the right granola bar for you and your fitness goals; some people want not to eat them. However, we offer something much more interesting: the option of making your granola bar.

Doing so is inexpensive, as the ingredients are likely to already be in your kitchen pantry. It gives the versatility of adapting the recipe to your personal preferences. It is also a food that you can make in batches and freeze for later. They can be as straightforward or as elaborate as you want them to be. However, to provide your body with the macronutrients it needs to enhance athletic performance, we'll keep this recipe short and sweet.

One of its' key ingredients is hemp, a superfood. It is a good source of omega 3, 6 and 9. It also has magnesium, manganese, iron and zinc. This ingredient is helpful for athletes, as it can help reduce pain in the tendons and ligaments. It also improves oxygen circulate more quickly in the bloodstream. In addition to this, hemp has anti-inflammatory properties, making it a great food to include in an athlete's diet.

Another nutrient-rich ingredient in this recipe is the date. Although this dry fruit has a higher number of calories, its' other health benefits make it an ingredient worth having in your diet. Dates have a low glycemic index. They are high in fiber, which helps digestive health and regulates bowel movement. It also slows digestion, which gives your body a greater control of blood sugar levels.

Dates are also high in antioxidants, which fight to reduce your risk of developing chronic disease. Some of the antioxidants found in dates are flavonoids, carotenoids and phenolic acid. These aid in reducing inflammation and in promoting cardiovascular health. Furthermore, dates are good for the human brain. We must not underestimate the usefulness of the brain in a workout, training and a big game. A healthy brain means improved memory, a better ability to learn and increased alertness. Moreover, dates make great natural sweeteners and can easily replace sugar in a recipe. Often, this is achieved by mixing dates with water to create a paste. If you need more convincing on how good dates are for you, know this. Dates help make for strong bones, too, because of nutrients like calcium, magnesium, phosphorus and potassium. In this instance, dates are being added to your granola bar. It will serve as the binding ingredient that holds your protein bar together. However, the versatility of this fruit makes it a great addition to sauces, salad dressings, marinades and oatmeal, too. In

Chapter 8. Lunch Recipes

Amazing Potato Dish

Preparation time: 10 minutes

Cooking time: 3 hours

Servings: 4

Ingredients:

1 and ½ pounds potatoes, peeled and roughly chopped

1 tablespoon olive oil

3 tablespoons water

1 small yellow onion, chopped

½ Cup veggie stock cube, crumbled

½ Teaspoon coriander, ground

½ Teaspoon cumin, ground

½ Teaspoon garam masala

½ Teaspoon chili powder

Black pepper to the taste

½ Pound spinach, roughly torn

Directions:

Put the potatoes in your slow cooker.

Add oil, water, onion, stock cube, coriander, cumin, garam masala, chili powder, black pepper and spinach.

Stir, cover and cook on High for 3 hours.

Divide into bowls and serve.

Enjoy!

Nutrition: calories 270, fat 4, fiber 6, carbs 8, protein 12

Textured Sweet Potatoes and Lentils Delight

Preparation time: 10 minutes

Cooking time: 4 hours and 30 minutes

Servings: 6

Ingredients:

6 cups sweet potatoes, peeled and cubed

2 teaspoons coriander, ground

2 teaspoons chili powder

1 yellow onion, chopped

3 cups veggie stock

4 garlic cloves, minced

A pinch of sea salt and black pepper

10 ounces canned coconut milk

1 cup water

1 and ½ cups red lentils

Directions:

Put sweet potatoes in your slow cooker.

Add coriander, chili powder, onion, stock, garlic, salt and pepper, stir, cover and cook on high for 3 hours.

Add lentils, stir, cover and cook for 1 hour and 30 minutes.

Add water and coconut milk, stir well, divide into bowls and serve right away.

Enjoy!

Nutrition: calories 300, fat 10, fiber 8, carbs 16, protein 10

Incredibly Tasty Pizza

Preparation time: 1 hour and 10 minutes

Cooking time: 1 hour and 45 minutes

Servings: 3

Ingredients:

For the dough:

½ Teaspoon italian seasoning

1 and ½ cups whole wheat flour

1 and ½ teaspoons instant yeast

1 tablespoon olive oil

A pinch of salt

½ Cup warm water

Cooking spray

For the sauce:

¼ Cup green olives, pitted and sliced

¼ Cup kalamata olives, pitted and sliced

½ Cup tomatoes, crushed

1 tablespoon parsley, chopped

1 tablespoon capers, rinsed

¼ Teaspoon garlic powder

¼ Teaspoon basil, dried

¼ Teaspoon oregano, dried

¼ Teaspoon palm sugar

¼ Teaspoon red pepper flakes

A pinch of salt and black pepper

½ Cup cashew mozzarella, shredded

Directions:

In your food processor, mix yeast with italian seasoning, a pinch of salt and flour.

Add oil and the water and blend well until you obtain a dough.

Transfer dough to a floured working surface, knead well, transfer to a greased bowl, cover and leave aside for 1 hour.

Meanwhile, in a bowl, mix green olives with kalamata olives, tomatoes, parsley, capers, garlic powder, oregano, sugar, salt, pepper and pepper flakes and stir well.

Transfer pizza dough to a working surface again and flatten it.

Shape so it will fit your slow cooker.

Grease your slow cooker with cooking spray and add dough.

Press well on the bottom.

Spread the sauce mix all over, cover and cook on high for 1 hour and 15 minutes.

Spread vegan mozzarella all over, cover again and cook on high for 30 minutes more.

Leave your pizza to cool down before slicing and serving it.

Nutrition: calories 340, fat 5, fiber 7, carbs 13, protein 15

Rich Beans Soup

Preparation time: 10 minutes

Cooking time: 7 hours

Servings: 4

Ingredients: 1 pound navy beans, 1 yellow onion, chopped

4 garlic cloves, crushed, 2 quarts veggie stock

A pinch of sea salt

Black pepper to the taste

2 potatoes, peeled and cubed

2 teaspoons dill, dried

1 cup sun-dried tomatoes, chopped

1 pound carrots, sliced, 4 tablespoons parsley, minced

Directions: Put the stock in your slow cooker. Add beans, onion, garlic, potatoes, tomatoes, carrots, dill, salt and pepper, stir, cover and cook on low for 7 hours. Stir your soup, add parsley, divide into bowls and serve. Enjoy!

Nutrition: calories 250, fat 4, fiber 3, carbs 9, protein 10

Delicious Baked Beans

Preparation time: 10 minutes

Cooking time: 12 hours

Servings: 8

Ingredients:

1 pound navy beans, soaked overnight and drained

1 cup maple syrup

1 cup bourbon

1 cup vegan bbq sauce

1 cup palm sugar

¼ Cup ketchup

1 cup water

¼ Cup mustard

¼ Cup blackstrap molasses

¼ Cup apple cider vinegar

¼ Cup olive oil

2 tablespoons coconut aminos

Directions:

Put the beans in your slow cooker.

Add maple syrup, bourbon, bbq sauce, sugar, ketchup, water, mustard, molasses, vinegar, oil and coconut aminos.

Stir everything, cover and cook on Low for 12 hours.

Divide into bowls and serve.

Enjoy!

Nutrition: calories 430, fat 7, fiber 8, carbs 15, protein 19

Indian Lentils

Preparation time: 10 minutes

Cooking time: 3 hours

Servings: 4

Ingredients:

1 yellow bell pepper, chopped

1 sweet potato, chopped

2 and ½ cups lentils, already cooked

4 garlic cloves, minced

1 yellow onion, chopped

2 teaspoons cumin, ground

15 ounces canned tomato sauce

½ Teaspoon ginger, ground

A pinch of cayenne pepper

1 tablespoons coriander, ground

1 teaspoon turmeric, ground

2 teaspoons paprika

2/3 cup veggie stock

1 teaspoon garam masala

A pinch of sea salt

Black pepper to the taste

Juice of 1 lemon

Directions:

Put the stock in your slow cooker.

Add potato, lentils, onion, garlic, cumin, bell pepper, tomato sauce, salt, pepper, ginger, coriander, turmeric, paprika, cayenne, garam masala and lemon juice.

Stir, cover and cook on high for 3 hours.

Stir your lentils mix again, divide into bowls and serve.

Enjoy!

Nutrition: calories 300, fat 6, fiber 5, carbs 9, protein 12

Delicious Butternut Squash Soup

Preparation time: 10 minutes

Cooking time: 6 hours

Servings: 8

Ingredients:

1 apple, cored, peeled and chopped

½ Pound carrots, chopped

1 pound butternut squash, peeled and cubed

1 yellow onion, chopped

A pinch of sea salt

Black pepper to the taste

1 bay leaf

3 cups veggie stock

14 ounces canned coconut milk

¼ Teaspoon sage, dried

Directions:

Put the stock in your slow cooker.

Add apple squash, carrots, onion, salt, pepper and bay leaf.

Stir, cover and cook on low for 6 hours.

Transfer to your blender, add coconut milk and sage and pulse really well.

Ladle into bowls and serve right away.

Enjoy!

Nutrition: calories 200, fat 3, fiber 6, carbs 8, protein 10

Amazing Mushroom Stew

Preparation time: 10 minutes

Cooking time: 8 hours

Servings: 4

Ingredients:

2 garlic cloves, minced

1 celery stalk, chopped

1 yellow onion, chopped

1 and ½ cups firm tofu, pressed and cubed

1 cup water

10 ounces mushrooms, chopped

1 pound mixed peas, corn and carrots

2 and ½ cups veggie stock

1 teaspoon thyme, dried

2 tablespoons coconut flour

A pinch of sea salt

Black pepper to the taste

Directions:

Put the water and stock in your slow cooker.

Add garlic, onion, celery, mushrooms, mixed veggies, tofu, thyme, salt, pepper and flour.

Stir everything, cover and cook on low for 8 hours.

Divide into bowls and serve hot.

Enjoy!

Nutrition: calories 230, fat 4, fiber 6, carbs 10, protein 7

Simple Tofu Dish

Preparation time: 10 minutes

Cooking time: 3 hours

Servings: 6

Ingredients:

1 big tofu package, cubed

1 tablespoon sesame oil

¼ Cup pineapple, cubed

1 tablespoon olive oil

2 garlic cloves, minced

1 tablespoons brown rice vinegar

2 teaspoon ginger, grated

¼ Cup soy sauce

5 big zucchinis, cubed

¼ Cup sesame seeds

Directions:

In your food processor, mix sesame oil with pineapple, olive oil, garlic, ginger, soy sauce and vinegar and whisk well.

Add this to your slow cooker and mix with tofu cubes.

Cover and cook on High for 2 hours and 45 minutes.

Add sesame seeds and zucchinis, stir gently, cover and cook on High for 15 minutes.

Divide between plates and serve.

Enjoy!

Nutrition: calories 200, fat 3, fiber 4, carbs 9, protein 10

Special Jambalaya

Preparation time: 10 minutes

Cooking time: 6 hours

Servings: 4

Ingredients:

6 ounces soy chorizo, chopped

1 and ½ cups celery ribs, chopped

1 cup okra

1 green bell pepper, chopped

16 ounces canned tomatoes and green chilies, chopped

2 garlic cloves, minced

½ Teaspoon paprika

1 and ½ cups veggie stock

A pinch of cayenne pepper

Black pepper to the taste

A pinch of salt

3 cups already cooked wild rice for serving

Directions:

Heat up a pan over medium high heat, add soy chorizo, stir, brown for a few minutes and transfer to your slow cooker.

Also, add celery, bell pepper, okra, tomatoes and chilies, garlic, paprika, salt, pepper and cayenne to your slow cooker.

Stir everything, add veggie stock, cover the slow cooker and cook on low for 6 hours.

Divide rice on plates, top each serving with your vegan jambalaya and serve hot.

Enjoy!

Nutrition: calories 150, fat 3, fiber 7, carbs 15, protein 9

Delicious Chard Soup

Preparation time: 10 minutes

Cooking time: 8 hours

Servings: 6

Ingredients:

1 yellow onion, chopped

1 tablespoon olive oil

1 celery stalk, chopped

2 garlic cloves, minced

1 carrot, chopped

1 bunch swiss chard, torn

1 cup brown lentils, dried

5 potatoes, peeled and cubed

1 tablespoon soy sauce

Black pepper to the taste

A pinch of sea salt

6 cups veggie stock

Directions:

Heat up a big pan with the oil over medium high heat, add onion, celery, garlic, carrot and Swiss chard, stir, cook for a few minutes and transfer to your slow cooker.

Also, add lentils, potatoes, soy sauce, salt, pepper and stock to the slow cooker, stir, cover and cook on Low for 8 hours.

Divide into bowls and serve hot.

Enjoy!

Nutrition: calories 200, fat 4, fiber 5, carbs 9, protein 12

Chinese Tofu and Veggies

Preparation time: 10 minutes

Cooking time: 4 hours

Servings: 4

Ingredients:

14 ounces extra firm tofu, pressed and cut into medium triangles

Cooking spray

2 teaspoons ginger, grated

1 yellow onion, chopped

3 garlic cloves, minced

8 ounces tomato sauce

¼ Cup hoisin sauce

¼ Teaspoon coconut aminos

2 tablespoons rice wine vinegar

1 tablespoon soy sauce

1 tablespoon spicy mustard

¼ Teaspoon red pepper, crushed

2 teaspoons molasses

2 tablespoons water

A pinch of black pepper

3 broccoli stalks

1 green bell pepper, cut into squares

2 zucchinis, cubed

Directions:

Heat up a pan over medium high heat, add tofu pieces, brown them for a few minutes and transfer to your slow cooker.

Heat up the pan again over medium high heat, add ginger, onion, garlic and tomato sauce, stir, sauté for a few minutes and transfer to your slow cooker as well.

Add hoisin sauce, aminos, vinegar, soy sauce, mustard, red pepper, molasses, water and black pepper, stir gently, cover and cook on high for 3 hours. Add zucchinis, bell pepper and broccoli, cover and cook on high for 1 more hour. Divide between plates and serve right away. Enjoy!

Nutrition: calories 300, fat 4, fiber 8, carbs 14, protein 13

Wonderful Corn Chowder

Preparation time: 10 minutes

Cooking time: 8 hours and 30 minutes

Servings: 6

Ingredients:

2 cups yellow onion, chopped

2 tablespoons olive oil

1 red bell pepper, chopped

1 pound gold potatoes, cubed

1 teaspoon cumin, ground

4 cups corn kernels

4 cups veggie stock

1 cup almond milk

A pinch of salt

A pinch of cayenne pepper

½ Teaspoon smoked paprika

Chopped scallions for serving

Directions:

Heat up a pan with the oil over medium heat, add onion, stir and sauté for 5 minutes and then transfer to your slow cooker.

Add bell pepper, 1 cup corn, potatoes, paprika, cumin, salt and cayenne, stir, cover and cook on low for 8 hours.

Blend this using an immersion blender and then mix with almond milk and the rest of the corn.

Stir chowder, cover and cook on low for 30 minutes more.

Ladle into bowls and serve with chopped scallions on top.

Enjoy!

Nutrition: calories 200, fat 4, fiber 7, carbs 13, protein 16

Black Eyed Peas Stew

Preparation time: 10 minutes

Cooking time: 4 hours

Servings: 8

Ingredients:

3 celery stalks, chopped

2 carrots, sliced

1 yellow onion, chopped

1 sweet potato, cubed

1 green bell pepper, chopped

3 cups black-eyed peas, soaked for 8 hours and drained

1 cup tomato puree

4 cups veggie stock

A pinch of salt

Black pepper to the taste

1 chipotle chile, minced

1 teaspoon ancho chili powder

1 teaspoons sage, dried and crumbled

2 teaspoons cumin, ground

Chopped coriander for serving

Directions:

Put celery in your slow cooker.

Add carrots, onion, potato, bell pepper, black-eyed peas, tomato puree, salt, pepper, chili powder, sage, chili, cumin and stock.

Stir, cover and cook on High for 4 hours.

Stir stew again, divide into bowls and serve with chopped coriander on top.

Enjoy!

Nutrition: calories 200, fat 4, fiber 7, carbs 9, protein 16

White Bean Cassoulet

Preparation time: 10 minutes

Cooking time: 6 hours

Servings: 4

Ingredients:

2 celery stalks, chopped

3 leeks, sliced

4 garlic cloves, minced

2 carrots, chopped

2 cups veggie stock

15 ounces canned tomatoes, chopped

1 bay leaf

1 tablespoon italian seasoning

30 ounces canned white beans, drained

For the breadcrumbs:

Zest from 1 lemon, grated

1 garlic clove, minced

2 tablespoons olive oil

1 cup vegan bread crumbs

¼ Cup parsley, chopped

Directions:

Heat up a pan with a splash of the veggie stock over medium heat, add celery and leeks, stir and cook for 2 minutes.

Add carrots and garlic, stir and cook for 1 minute more.

Add this to your slow cooker and mix with stock, tomatoes, bay leaf, italian seasoning and beans.

Stir, cover and cook on low for 6 hours.

Meanwhile, heat up a pan with the oil over medium high heat, add bread crumbs, lemon zest, 1 garlic clove and parsley, stir and toast for a couple of minutes.

Divide your white beans mix into bowls, sprinkle bread crumbs mix on top and serve.

Enjoy!

Nutrition: calories 223, fat 3, fiber 7, carbs 10, protein 7

Light Jackfruit Dish

Preparation time: 10 minutes

Cooking time: 6 hours

Servings: 4

Ingredients:

40 ounces green jackfruit in brine, drained

½ Cup agave nectar

½ Cup gluten free tamari sauce

¼ Cup soy sauce

1 cup white wine

2 tablespoons ginger, grated

8 garlic cloves, minced

1 pear, cored and chopped

1 yellow onion, chopped

½ Cup water

4 tablespoons sesame oil

Directions:

Put jackfruit in your slow cooker.

Add agave nectar, tamari sauce, soy sauce, wine, ginger, garlic, pear, onion, water and oil.

Stir well, cover and cook on low for 6 hours.

Divide jackfruit mix into bowls and serve.

Enjoy!

Nutrition: calories 160, fat 4, fiber 1, carbs 10, protein 3

Veggie Curry

Preparation time: 10 minutes

Cooking time: 4 hours

Servings: 4

Ingredients:

1 tablespoon ginger, grated

14 ounces canned coconut milk

Cooking spray

16 ounces firm tofu, pressed and cubed

1 cup veggie stock

¼ Cup green curry paste

½ Teaspoon turmeric

1 tablespoon coconut sugar

1 yellow onion, chopped

1 and ½ cup red bell pepper, chopped

A pinch of salt

¾ Cup peas

1 eggplant, chopped

Directions:

Put the coconut milk in your slow cooker.

Add ginger, stock, curry paste, turmeric, sugar, onion, bell pepper, salt, peas and eggplant pieces, stir, cover and cook on high for 4 hours.

Meanwhile, spray a pan with cooking spray and heat up over medium high heat.

Add tofu pieces and brown them for a few minutes on each side.

Divide tofu into bowls, add slowly cooked curry mix on top and serve.

Enjoy!

Nutrition: calories 200, fat 4, fiber 6, carbs 10, protein 9

Chapter 9. Burger And Sandwiches

Spicy Chickpea Sandwich

Preparation time: 10 minutes

Cooking time: 40 minutes

Servings: 4

Ingredients:

Raisins (.25 C.)

Spinach Leaves (.50 C.)

Red Onion (.50)

Red Pepper (.50)

Ground Cumin (.50 t.)

Turmeric (.25 t.)

Garam Masala Powder (1 T.)

Olive Oil (2 T.)

Garlic (1)

Chickpeas (14 Oz.)

Fresh Coriander (4 T.)

Salt (.25 t.)

Bread (8 Slices)

Directions:

To start, you will want to get out your blender. When you are set, add in the chickpeas, olive oil, juice of one lemon, and garlic clove. Blend everything together until the ingredients create a chunky paste.

With the chickpea paste made, transfer it into a bowl and mix in the cumin powder, turmeric, and the curry powder. Give everything a good stir to make sure there are no chunks in your chickpea paste.

Next, add in chopped onion and red pepper into the paste. At this point, you can also add in the chopped coriander and raisins. If you would like, feel free to season with salt and lemon juice at this point as well.

Finally, take your bread, spread the chickpea mix, top with some spinach leaves, and enjoy a nice protein packed sandwich!

Nutrition:

Calories: 280 Protein: 8g Fat: 8g

Carbs: 48g Fibers: 8g

Baked Spicy Tofu Sandwich

Preparation time: 10 minutes

Cooking time: 45 minutes

Servings: 4

Ingredients:

Whole Grain Bread (8)

Maple Syrup (1 T.)

White Miso Paste (1 T.)

Tomato Paste (1 T.)

Liquid Smoke (1 Dash)

Soy Sauce (1 T.)

Cumin (1 t.)

Paprika (.50 t.)

Chipotles in Adobo Sauce (1 t.)

Vegetable Broth (1 C.)

Tofu (16 Oz.)

Tomato (1)

Chopped Red Onion (.25 C.)

Tabasco (1 Dash)

Lime (1)

Cumin (.25 t.)

Chili Powder (.25 t.)

Coriander (.25 t.)

Cilantro (.25 C.)

Avocado (1)

Ground Black Pepper (.25 t.)

Garlic (2)

Lime (.50)

Directions:

To Prepare for this recipe, you will want to Preparation your tofu the night before. To start, you will want to press the tofu for a few hours. Once this is done, cut the tofu into eight slices and then place them in the freezer.

When you are ready, it is time to make the marinade for the tofu. To do this, take a bowl and mix together the vegetable broth, tomato paste, maple syrup, and all of the spices from the list above. Be sure to stir everything together to get the spices spread through the vegetable broth. Once it is mixed together, add in your thawed slices of tofu and soak them for a few hours.

Once the tofu is marinated, heat your oven to 425 degrees. When the oven is warm, place the tofu on a baking sheet and place in the oven for twenty minutes. At the end of this time, the tofu should be nice and crispy on the top and edges.

When your tofu is cooked to your liking, layer it on your bread slices with your favorite toppings. This sandwich can be enjoyed cold or warm!

Nutrition:

Calories: 390

Protein: 21g

Fat: 16g

Carbs: 49g

Fibers: 11g

Lentil Burgers

Preparation time: 10 minutes

Cooking time: 15 minutes

Servings: 4

Ingredients:

Bread Crumbs (2 T.)

Crushed Walnuts (2 T.)

Soy Sauce (1 t.)

Cooked Lentils (2 C.)

Salt (.50 t.)

Cumin (.25 t.)

Nutritional Yeast (.25 C.)

Directions:

First, you will want to cook your two cups of lentils. You will want to complete this task following the Preparation provided on the side of the package. Once this step is complete, drain the lentils and place them into a medium-sized bowl. When the lentils are in place, gently mash them until they reach a smooth consistency.

At this point, you will want to add in the bread crumbs, crushed walnuts, soy sauce, nutritional yeast, cumin, and the salt. Be sure to mix everything together and then begin to form your patties. They should be about four inches in diameter and only an inch thick.

With your patties formed, you will want to heat a medium size pan over medium heat and begin to warm it. Once warm, add in oil and cook each patty for two to three minutes on each side. By the end, each side of the burger should be crisp and brown.

Finally, serve on a warm bun with your favorite vegan condiments and garnish!

Nutrition: Calories: 410, Protein: 31g, Fat: 5g, Carbs: 65g, Fibers: 33g

Sweet Hawaiian Burger

Preparation time: 10 minutes

Cooking time: 15 minutes

Servings: 4

Ingredients:

Panko Breadcrumbs (1 C.)

Red Kidney Beans (14 Oz.)

Vegetable Oil (1 T.)

Diced Sweet Potato (1.50 C.)

Minced Garlic (1)

Soy Sauce (2 T.)

Apple Cider Vinegar (3 T.)

Maple Syrup (.50 C.)

Water (.50 C.)

Tomato Paste (.50 C.)

Pineapple Rings (4)

Salt (.25 t.)

Pepper (.25 t.)

Cayenne (.10 t.)

Ground Cumin (1.50 t.)

Burger Buns (4)

Optional: Red Onion, Tomato, Lettuce, Vegan Mayo

Directions:

First, you will want to heat your oven to 400 degrees. As the oven warms up, take your sweet potato and toss it in oil. When this step is complete, place the diced sweet potato pieces in a single layer on a baking sheet. Once this is done, pop the sheet into the oven and cook for about twenty minutes. Halfway through, flip the pieces over to assure the sweet potato cooks all the way through. When this is done, remove the sheet from the oven and allow the sweet potato to cool down slightly.

Next, you will want to get out your food processor. When you are ready, add in the beans, sweet potatoes, breadcrumbs, cayenne, cumin, soy sauce, garlic, and onion pieces. Once in place, begin to pulse the ingredients together until you have a finely chopped mixture. As you do this, season the "dough" with pepper and salt as desired. Now, shape the dough into four patties.

When your patties are formed, begin to heat a large skillet over medium heat. As the pan warms up, place your oil and then grill each side of your patties. Typically, this will take five to six minutes on each side. You will know the burger is cooked through when it is browned on each side.

All you need to do now is assemble your burger! If you want, try baking the pineapple rings—three minutes on each side should do the trick! Top your burger with lettuce, tomato, and vegan mayo for some extra flavor.

Nutrition:

Calories: 460

Protein: 15g

Fat: 12g

Carbs: 80g

Fibers: 6g

Tofu & Veggie Burgers

Preparation time: 20 minutes

Cooking time: 8 minutes

Servings: 2

Ingredients

Patties

½ cup firm tofu, pressed and drained

1 medium carrot, peeled and grated

1 tablespoon onion, chopped

1 tablespoon scallion, chopped

1 tablespoon fresh parsley, chopped

½ garlic clove, minced

2 teaspoons low-sodium soy sauce

1 tablespoon cornflour

1 teaspoon nutritional yeast flakes

½ teaspoon Dijon mustard

1 teaspoon paprika

¼ teaspoon ground turmeric

½ teaspoon ground black pepper

2 tablespoons canola oil

For Serving

1 small avocado, peeled, pitted, and sliced

½ cup cherry tomatoes, halved

2 cup fresh baby greens

How to Prepare

For patties: in a bowl, add the tofu and with a fork, mash well.

Add the remaining ingredients (except for oil) and mix until well combined.

Make 4 equal-sized patties from the mixture.

Heat the oil in a frying pan over low heat and cook the patties for about 4 minutes per side.

Divide the avocado, tomatoes, and greens onto serving plates.

Top each plate with 2 patties and serve.

Nutrition

Calories 342   Total Fat 28.5 g   Saturated Fat 4 g

Cholesterol 0 mg   Sodium 335 mg   Total Carbs 17.7 g

Fiber 7.7 g   Sugar 4.5 g   Protein 10 g

Buckwheat Burgers

Preparation time: 20 minutes

Cooking time: 45 minutes

Total time: 1 hour 5 minutes

Servings: 2

Ingredients

Patties

¾ cup dry buckwheat

1½ cups water

Salt, to taste

2 tablespoons olive oil, divided

½ of large yellow onion, chopped finely

½ of large carrot, peeled and grated

½ celery stalk, chopped finely

1 fresh kale leaf, tough ribs removed and chopped finely

1 large cooked sweet potato, mashed

2 tablespoons almond butter

2 tablespoons low-sodium soy sauce

For Serving

3 cups fresh baby greens

1 cup cherry tomatoes, halved

1 cup purple cabbage, shredded

1 yellow bell pepper, seeded and sliced

How to Prepare

Preheat oven to 350°F and line a baking sheet with parchment paper.

For patties: heat a non-stick frying pan over medium heat and toast the buckwheat for about 5 minutes, stirring continuously.

Add the water and salt and bring to a boil over high heat.

Reduce the heat to low and cook, covered for about 15 minutes or until all the water is absorbed.

Meanwhile, heat 1 tablespoon of the oil in a skillet over medium heat and sauté the onion for about 4–5 minutes.

Add the carrot and celery and cook for about 5 minutes.

Stir in the remaining ingredients and remove from the heat.

Transfer the mixture into a bowl with buckwheat and stir to combine.

Set aside to cool completely.

Make 4 equal-sized patties from the mixture.

Arrange the patties onto the Prepared baking sheet in a single layer and bake for about 20 minutes per side.

Divide the greens, tomatoes, cabbage, and bell pepper onto serving plates.

Top each plate with 2 patties and serve

Nutrition

Calories 588   Total Fat 25.2 g   Saturated Fat 3.1 g

Cholesterol 0 mg   Sodium 1000 mg   Total Carbs 84.8 g

Fiber 15.4 g   Sugar 16.4 g   Protein 16.7 g

Chapter 10.   Dinner Recipes

Green Curry Tofu

Preparation time: 10 minutes

Cooking time: 15 minutes

Servings: 1

Ingredients:

Lime Juice (1 T.)

Tamari Sauce (1 T.)

Water Chestnuts (8 Oz.)

Green Beans (1 C.)

Salt (.50 t.)

Vegetable Broth (.50 C.)

Coconut Milk (14 Oz.)

Chickpeas (1 C.)

Green Curry Paste (3 T.)

Frozen Edamame (1 C.)

Garlic Cloves (2)

Ginger (1 inch)

Olive Oil (1 t.)

Diced Onion (1)

Extra-firm Tofu (8 Oz.)

Brown Basmati Rice (1 C.)

Directions:

To start, you will want to cook your rice according to the Preparation on the package. You can do this in a rice cooker or simply on top of the stove.

Next, you will want to Prepare your tofu. You can remove the tofu from the package and set it on a plate. Once in place, set another plate on top and something heavy so you can begin to drain the tofu. Once the tofu is Prepared, cut it into half inch cubes.

Next, take a medium-sized pan and place it over medium heat. As the pan heats up, go ahead and place your olive oil. When the olive oil begins to sizzle, add your onions and cook until they turn a nice translucent color. Typically, this process will take about five minutes. When your onions are ready, add in the garlic and ginger. With these in place, cook the ingredients for another two to three minutes.

Once the last step is done, add in your curry paste and edamame. Cook these two ingredients until the edamame is no longer frozen.

With these ready, you will now add in the cubed tofu, chickpeas, vegetable broth, coconut milk, and the salt. When everything is in place, you will want to bring the pot to a simmer. Add in the water chestnuts and green beans next and cook for a total of five minutes.

When all of the ingredients are cooked through, you can remove the pan from the heat and divide your meal into bowls. For extra flavor, try stirring in tamari, lime juice, or soy sauce. This recipe is excellent served over rice or any other side dish!

Nutrition: Calories: 760, Protein: 23g, Fat: 38g

Carbs: 89g, Fibers: 9g

African Peanut Protein Stew

Preparation time: 10 minutes

Cooking time: 30 minutes

Servings: 4

Ingredients:

Basmati Rice (1 Package)

Roasted Peanuts (.25 C.)

Baby Spinach (2 C.)

Chickpeas (15 Oz.)

Chili Powder (1.50 t.)

Vegetable Broth (4 C.)

Natural Peanut Butter (.33 C.)

Pepper (.25 t.)

Salt (.25 t.)

Diced Tomatoes (28 Oz.)

Chopped Sweet Potato (1)

Diced Jalapeno (1)

Diced Red Pepper (1)

Sweet Onion (1)

Olive Oil (1 t.)

Directions:

First, you will want to cook your onion. You will do this by heating olive oil in a large saucepan over medium heat. Once the olive oil is sizzling, add in the onion and cook for five minutes or so. The onion will turn translucent when it is cooked through.

With the onion done, you will now add in the canned tomatoes, diced sweet potato, jalapeno, and bell peppers. Simmer all of these ingredients over a medium to high heat for about five minutes. If desired, you can season these vegetables with salt and pepper.

As the vegetables cook, you will want to make your sauce. You will do this by taking a bowl and mix together one cup of vegetable broth with the peanut butter. Be sure to mix well, so there are no clumps. Once this is done, pour the sauce into the saucepan along with three more cups of vegetable broth. At this point, you will want to season the dish with cayenne and chili powder.

Next, cover your pan and reduce to a lower heat. Go ahead and allow these ingredients to simmer for about ten to twenty minutes. At the end of this time, the sweet potato should be nice and tender.

Last, you will want to add in the spinach and chickpeas. Give everything a good stir to mix together. You will want to cook this dish until the spinach begins to wilt. Once again, you can add salt and pepper as needed.

Finally, serve your dish over rice, garnish with peanuts, and enjoy!

Nutrition:

Calories: 440

Protein: 16g

Fat: 13g

Carbs: 69g

Fibers: 12g

Thai Zucchini Noodle Salad

Preparation time: 10 minutes

Cooking time: 35 minutes

Servings: 4

Ingredients:

Peanuts (.50 C.)

Peanut Sauce (.50 C.), Water (2 T.)

Extra-firm Tofu (.50 Block)

Chopped Green Onions (.25 C.)

Spiralized Carrot (1), Spiralized Zucchini (3)

Directions: First, you are going to want to create your peanut sauce. To do this, take a small bowl and slowly mix your peanut sauce with water. You will want to add one tablespoon at a time to achieve the thickness you desire. Next, you will combine all of the ingredients from above, minus the peanuts, into a large mixing bowl. Once everything is in place, top with the salad dressing and give everything a good toss to assure even coating. Finally, sprinkle your peanuts on top, and your meal is done!

Nutrition: Calories: 200, Protein: 13g, Fat: 13g, Carbs: 11g, Fibers: 5g

Split Pea and Cauliflower Stew

Preparation time: 10 minutes

Cooking time: 60 minutes

Servings: 4

Ingredients:

Green Onions (.25 C.)

Chopped Cilantro (.25 C.)

Salt (1.50 t.)

Garam Masala (1 t.)

Apple Cider Vinegar (2 t.)

Light Coconut Milk (15 Oz.)

Vegetable Broth (2 C.)

Ground Turmeric (1 t.)

Curry Powder (3 t.)

Minced Garlic (6)

Chopped Carrots (2)

Chopped Onion (1)

Cumin Seeds (1 t.)

Mustard Seeds (1 t.)

Spinach Leaves (3 C.)

Chopped Cauliflower (1)

Cooked Split Peas (2 C.)

Directions:

Before you begin cooking this recipe, you will want to Prepare your split peas according to the Preparation on their package.

Once your split peas are cooked, you will want to preheat your oven to 375 degrees. Once warm, place your chopped cauliflower pieces onto a baking sheet and pop it into the oven for ten to fifteen minutes. By the end, the cauliflower should be tender and slightly brown.

Next, you will want to place a large pot on your stove and turn the heat to medium. As the pot heats up, add in the oil, cumin seeds, and mustard seeds. Within sixty seconds, the seeds will begin popping. You will want to make sure you are stirring these ingredients frequently, so they do not burn.

Now that the seeds and oil are warm, you can add in your onion, garlic, ginger, and chopped carrots. Cook these for five minutes or until the carrot and onion are nice and soft. Once they are, you can add in your turmeric and curry powder. Be sure to gently mix everything together so you can evenly coat the vegetables.

After one minute of allowing the vegetables to soak up the spices, you will want to add in the coconut milk, split peas, and vegetable broth. At this point, you will want to lower the heat to low and place a cover over your pot. Allow all of the ingredients to simmer for about twenty minutes. As everything cooks, be sure to stir the pot occasionally to make sure nothing sticks to the bottom.

Finally, you will want to stir in the garam masala, apple cider vinegar, and the roasted cauliflower. If needed, you can also add salt as desired. When these ingredients are in place, go ahead and allow the stew to simmer for another ten minutes or so.

As a final touch, feel free to top your stew with green onions and chopped cilantro for extra flavors!

Nutrition: Calories: 700, Protein: 31g, Fat: 31g, Carbs: 84g, Fibers: 34g

Black Bean and Pumpkin Chili

Preparation time: 10 minutes

Cooking time: 15 minutes

Servings: 4

Ingredients:

Garbanzo Beans (1 Can)

Black Beans (1 Can)

Vegetable Stock (1 C.)

Tomatoes (1 C.)

Pumpkin Puree (1 C.)

Chopped Onion (1)

Olive Oil (1 T.)

Chili Powder (2 T.)

Cumin Powder (1 T.)

Salt (.25 t.)

Pepper (.25 t.)

Directions:

To begin, you will want to place a large pot over medium heat. At the pot warms up, place your olive oil, garlic, and chopped onion into the bottom. Allow this mixture to cook for about five minutes or until the onion is soft.

At this point, you will now want to add in the garbanzo beans, black beans, vegetable stock, canned tomatoes, and pumpkin. If you do not have any vegetable stock on hand, you can also use water.

With your ingredients in place, add in the half of the chili powder, half of the cumin, and any salt and pepper according to your own taste. Once the spices are in place, give the chili a quick taste and add more as needed.

Now, bring the pot to a boil and stir all of the ingredients together to assure the spices are spread evenly throughout your dish.

Last, bring the pot to a simmer and cook everything for about twenty minutes. When the twenty minutes are done, remove the pot from the heat, and enjoy!

Nutrition: Calories: 390, Protein: 19g, Fat: 8g, Carbs: 65g, Fibers: 21g

Matcha Tofu Soup

Preparation time: 10 minutes

Cooking time: 55 minutes

Servings: 4

Ingredients:

Vegetable Broth (.5 0 C.)

Extra-firm Tofu (1 Package)

Light Coconut Milk (13.5 Oz.)

Kale (5 C.)

Garlic Powder (.25 t.)

Smoked Paprika (.25 t)

Ground Black Pepper (.25 t.)

Mirin (1 t.)

Soy Sauce (2 T.)

Cilantro (1 C.)

Matcha Powder (2 t.)

Vegetable Broth (4 C.)

Ground Black Pepper (.25 t.)

Cayenne Pepper (.25 t.)

Garlic (1 t.)

Minced Garlic (3)

Chopped Potato (1)

Chopped Onion (1)

Directions:

To start, you will want to place a large pot over medium heat. As the pot warms up, add a splash of vegetable broth to the bottom and begin to cook the chopped potato and onion. Typically, it will take eight to ten minutes until they are nice and soft. When the vegetables are ready, you can then add in the black pepper, cayenne pepper, ginger, and garlic. Sauté these ingredients for another minute.

When these vegetables are Prepared, you can add in the kale and cook for a few more minutes. Once the kale begins to wilt, stir in the rest of the vegetable broth and bring your soup to a boil. Once boiling, reduce the heat, cover the pot, and simmer all of the ingredients for thirty minutes. After fifteen minutes, remove the top so you can stir in the matcha and cilantro.

Once the thirty minutes are done, remove the pot from the heat and allow the soup to cool for a little. Once cool, place the mixture into a blender and gently stir in the coconut milk. Blend the soup on high until you reach a silky and smooth consistency for the soup.

Finally, cook your tofu according to your own preference. Be sure to chop the tofu into cubes and brown on all sides. Once cooked, place the tofu in your soup and enjoy!

Nutrition: Calories: 450, Protein: 20g, Fat: 32g, Carbs: 27g, Fibers: 7g

Sweet Potato Tomato Soup

Preparation time: 10 minutes

Cooking time: 15 minutes

Servings: 4

Ingredients:

Water or Vegetable Stock (1 L.)

Tomato Puree (2 T.)

Garlic (3)

Chopped Onion (1)

Red Lentils (1 C.)

Chopped Carrots (3)

Chopped Sweet Potato (1)

Salt (.25 t.)

Pepper (.25 t.)

Ginger (.50 t.)

Chili Powder (.50 t.)

Directions:

First, we are going to prepare the vegetables for this recipe. You will do this by preheating your oven to 350 degrees. While the oven heats up, you will want to peel and cut both your sweet potato and the carrots. Once they are prepared, place them on a baking sheet and drizzle them with olive oil. You can also add salt and pepper if you would like. When you are ready, place the sheet into the oven for forty minutes. By the end, the vegetables should be nice and soft.

As the sweet potato and carrots get baked in the oven, place a medium-sized pan over medium heat and begin to cook your garlic and onion. After five minutes or so, you will want to add in your cooked lentils, tomato, and the spices from the list above. By the end, the lentils should be soft.

Finally, you will add all of the ingredients into a blender and blend until the soup if perfectly smooth.

Nutrition:

Calories: 350   Protein: 16g

Fat: 11g   Carbs: 48g   Fibers: 19g

Baked Spicy Tofu Sandwich

Preparation time: 10 minutes

Cooking time: 45 minutes

Servings: 4

Ingredients:

Whole Grain Bread (8)

Maple Syrup (1 T.)

White Miso Paste (1 T.)

Tomato Paste (1 T.)

Liquid Smoke (1 Dash)

Soy Sauce (1 T.)

Cumin (1 t.)

Paprika (.50 t.)

Chipotles in Adobo Sauce (1 t.)

Vegetable Broth (1 C.)

Tofu (16 Oz.)

Tomato (1)

Chopped Red Onion (.25 C.)

Tabasco (1 Dash)

Lime (1)

Cumin (.25 t.)

Chili Powder (.25 t.)

Coriander (.25 t.)

Cilantro (.25 C.)

Avocado (1)

Ground Black Pepper (.25 t.)

Garlic (2)

Lime (.50)

Directions:

To prepare for this recipe, you will want to prep your tofu the night before. To start, you will want to press the tofu for a few hours. Once this is done, cut the tofu into eight slices and then place them in the freezer.

When you are ready, it is time to make the marinade for the tofu. To do this, take a bowl and mix together the vegetable broth, tomato paste, maple syrup, and all of the spices from the list above. Be sure to stir everything together to get the spices spread through the vegetable broth. Once it is mixed together, add in your thawed slices of tofu and soak them for a few hours.

Once the tofu is marinated, heat your oven to 425 degrees. When the oven is warm, place the tofu on a baking sheet and place in the oven for twenty minutes. At the end of this time, the tofu should be nice and crispy on the top and edges.

When your tofu is cooked to your liking, layer it on your bread slices with your favorite toppings. This sandwich can be enjoyed cold or warm!

Nutrition:

Calories: 390

Protein: 21g

Fat: 16g

Carbs: 49g

Fibers: 11g

Vegetable Stir-Fry

Preparation time: 10 minutes

Cooking time: 45 minutes

Servings: Three

Ingredients:

Zucchini (.50)

Red Bell Pepper (.50)

Broccoli (.50)

Red Cabbage (1 C.)

Brown Rice (.50 C.)

Tamari Sauce (2 T.)

Red Chili Pepper (1)

Fresh Parsley (.25 t.)

Garlic (4)

Olive Oil (2 T.)

Optional: Sesame Seeds

Directions:

To begin, you will want to cook your brown rice according to the directions that are placed on the package. Once this step is done, place the brown rice in a bowl and put it to the side.

Next, you will want to take a frying pan and place some water in the bottom. Bring the pan over medium heat and then add in your chopped vegetables. Once in place, cook the vegetables for five minutes or until they are tender.

When the vegetables are cooked through, you will then want to add in the parsley, cayenne powder, and the garlic. You will want to cook this mixture for a minute or so. Be sure you stir the ingredients so that nothing sticks to the bottom of your pan.

Now, add in the rice and tamari to your pan. You will cook this mixture for a few more minutes or until everything is warmed through.

For extra flavor, try adding sesame seeds before you enjoy your lunch! If you have any leftovers, you can keep this stir-fry in a sealed container for about five days in your fridge.

Nutrition:

Calories: 280   Protein: 10g

Fat: 12g   Carbs: 38g   Fibers: 6g

Creamy Tomato Lentil Soup

Preparation Time: 10 minutes

Cooking Time: 35 minutes

Servings: 4

Ingredients:

1 medium yellow onion, chopped

2 bay leaves

½ tsp. sea salt

½ tsp. black pepper

3 medium tomato, chopped

1/3 cup coconut milk

1/3 cup tomato paste

1 cup mixed lentils

1 cup vegetable broth

1 tsp. paprika

3 tbsp. olive oil

Method:

Heat oil in a medium-sized pot, and once hot, add the onion to it. Cook them for 5 minutes or until softened. Stir in the lentils, paprika and bay leaves to the pot and cook for 2 minutes or until fragrant. Add tomato paste, vegetable stock and chopped tomato to it. Bring the stock mixture to boiling and allow it to cook for 15 to 20 minutes. Tip: add water if it seems dry. Taste to season, and add more salt and pepper as needed.

Before serving, swirl the coconut milk over it. Serve it hot. Tip: You can also blend in a high-speed blender for a smoother soup.

Nutritional Information Per Serving: Calories: 346Kcal

Protein: 15g Carbohydrates: 42g Fat: 15g

Chili Carne

Preparation Time: 10 minutes

Cooking Time: 40 minutes

Servings: 6

Ingredients:

2 celery stalks, chopped finely

Salt and pepper, to taste

2 tbsp. oil

1 tsp. chili powder

2 carrots, chopped

3 ½ oz. split red lentils

3 garlic cloves, minced

14 oz. soy mince

1 large red onion, sliced thinly

14 oz. red kidney beans, drained and washed

1 tsp. cumin, ground

2 red peppers, chopped finely

1 ¾ lb. chopped tomatoes

1 cup vegetable stock

Method:

Heat oil in a large-sized skillet.

When the oil is hot, stir in the onion, peppers, garlic, carrot and celery, and sauté them for 3 minutes or until softened.

Spoon in cumin, chili powder, pepper and salt. Mix.

Add chopped tomatoes, soy mince, vegetable stock, kidney beans and lentils. Combine well.

Bring the mixture to a simmer.

Taste for seasoning and add more salt and pepper as needed.

Serve hot.

Tip: Pair it with basmati rice and a squeeze of lime juice.

Nutritional Information Per Serving: Calories: 340Kcal

Protein: 25g Carbohydrates: 42g Fat: 8g

Mexican Lentil Stew

Preparation Time: 10 minutes

Cooking Time: 45 minutes

Servings: 6

Ingredients:

½ tsp. salt

1 yellow onion, diced

8 cups vegetable broth

1 avocado, diced

2 carrots, peeled and diced

2 cups lentils, (preferably green) washed

1 red bell pepper, diced

2 tbsp. extra virgin olive oil

1 tbsp. cumin

2 celery stalks, diced

Cilantro, as needed, for garnishing

3 garlic cloves, minced

¼ tsp. smoked paprika

2 × 4 oz. diced green chili

1 tsp. oregano

2 cups diced tomatoes

Method:

You need to heat oil in a large pot over medium heat.

When the oil is hot, stir in the bell pepper, onion, celery and carrot.

Sauté them for 4 to 5 minutes or until softened.

Next, spoon in garlic, oregano, cumin and paprika. Mix and cook for a minute.

Stir in lentils, tomatoes, chili, broth and salt to it. Bring the mixture to a boil.

Simmer the stew for 30 to 40 minutes or until the lentils are tender. Keep the lid tilted.

Taste for seasoning and add more salt and pepper as needed.

Serve it hot.

Tip: Top with coriander and avocado slices.

Nutritional Information Per Serving:

Calories: 429Kcal

Protein: 25.1g

Carbohydrates: 51.9g

Fat: 14.2g

Lentil Meatloaf

Preparation Time: 10 minutes

Cooking Time: 45 minutes

Servings: 4 to 6

Ingredients:

1 cup green lentils

½ tsp. salt

2 cups water

1 tsp. basil, dried

¼ tsp. pepper

1 tsp. olive oil

1 tsp. garlic powder

2 tbsp. flaxseeds

4 tbsp. water

1 cup tomato sauce

1 yellow onion, diced

1 cup regular steel cut oats

1 tsp. parsley, dried

¼ cup BBQ sauce

2 tbsp. ketchup

Method:

Boil water in a pot over medium-high heat.

Once boiling, add the lentils and cook them for 30 minutes or until cooked. Drain the water and mash the lentils slightly. Transfer to a bowl and allow to cool.Combine the flaxseed with the water in another bowl and set it aside for 15 minutes. Heat oil in a medium-sized skillet over medium heat.

Stir in the onion and cook for 4 to 5 minutes or until softened. Next, add the onion and oats to the lentils along with the remaining ingredients, apart from the BBQ sauce and ketchup. Stir well until everything comes together. Transfer the dough to a well-greased loaf pan and smooth out the top. Spoon the ketchup and BBQ sauce over it. Bake for 43 to 45 minutes at 350°F or until it is golden brown and firm. Tip: Top with additional BBQ sauce if desired.

Nutritional Information Per Serving: Calories: 987Kcal

Protein: 34g Carbohydrates: 165g Fat: 26g

Black Bean Soup

Preparation Time: 10 minutes

Cooking Time: 25 minutes

Servings: 6

Ingredients:

4 cups black beans, cooked

1 medium onion, diced

14 ½ oz. diced tomatoes

2 garlic cloves, minced

4 cups vegetable broth

1 tsp. cumin

1 red bell pepper, diced

½ tsp. oregano, dried

½ tsp. salt

½ tsp. smoked paprika

Method:

Begin by heating a pot over a medium-high heat.

When hot, stir in the onion, red bell pepper and garlic along with ¼ cup of water.

Cook for 6 minutes or until the veggies have softened

Stir in the seasoning and cook for another 2 minutes

Add beans, vegetable broth and tomato BBQ to it. Combine.

Bring the broth mixture to a boil and lower the heat to sim.

Allow it to simmer for 20 minutes.

Finally, pour the soup into a high-speed blender.

Tip: Top with additional BBQ sauce.

Nutritional Information Per Serving:

Calories: 987Kcal

Protein: 34g

Carbohydrates: 165g

Mushroom Pasta

Preparation Time: 10 minutes

Cooking Time: 30 minutes

Servings: 6

Ingredients:

2 green onions, sliced thinly

12 oz. mixed mushrooms, sliced thinly

1 lb. linguine

3 garlic cloves, chopped finely

½ tsp. salt

¼ cup nutritional yeast

6 tbsp. oil

¾ tsp. black pepper, ground

Method:

Cook the linguine by following the instructions on the packet.

Once the pasta is cooked, reserve ¾ cup of the pasta water. Drain the remaining water and transfer the cooked pasta into a pot.

Spoon oil into a large saucepan and heat it over medium-high heat.

Stir in the mushrooms and garlic.

Sauté for 4 minutes or until the mushrooms become tender. Stir frequently.

Combine the mushrooms with the linguine, nutritional yeast, salt, pepper and ¾ cup of the water. Mix until everything comes together.

Garnish it with green onions. Tip: You could try adding bell peppers to the dish.

Nutritional Information Per Serving: Calories: 430Kcal

Protein: 15g Carbohydrates: 62g Fat: 15g

Lemon Pasta Alfredo

Preparation Time: 10 minutes

Cooking Time: 35 minutes

Servings: 4

Ingredients:

3 tbsp. almonds, blanched & sliced

12 oz. eggless pasta

1 tsp. lemon zest, finely grated

2 cups almond milk, unsweetened

2 tbsp. extra virgin olive oil

4 oz. soy cream cheese

3 garlic cloves, minced

Salt and black Pepper, as needed

3 tbsp. nutritional yeast plus for garnishing

½ cup fresh parsley, chopped

Method:

Cook the pasta in a pot of boiling water over a medium-high heat by following the instructions given in the packet. Drain the water, keeping 1 cup of the pasta water aside.

Put the nutritional yeast, ¼ teaspoon pepper, almond milk, one teaspoon salt, soy cream cheese, almonds into a blender.

Blend for 2 minutes or until smooth.

Spoon in oil and garlic to a large skillet and heat it over a medium-high heat.

Cook for one minute or until the garlic is aromatic.

Stir in the almond milk mixture along with ½ cup of the reserved pasta water.

Bring the mixture to a gentle boil and allow it to simmer for 6 to 8 minutes or until thick and creamy. Remove the skillet from the stove and add the pasta. Mix well. Tip: If it seems too thickened, add a bit of water. Transfer the mixture to the serving bowls and garnish with parsley and nutritional yeast. Tip: Instead of almonds, you can also use walnuts.

Nutritional Information Per Serving: Calories: 520Kcal

Protein: 22g Carbohydrates: 74g Fat: 15g

Chapter 11. Dessert And Snacks

Banana-Nut Bread Bars

Preparation time: 5 minutes

Cooking time: 30 minutes

Servings: 9 bars

Ingredients

Nonstick cooking spray (optional)

2 large ripe bananas

1 tablespoon maple syrup

½ Teaspoon vanilla extract

2 cups old-fashioned rolled oats

½ Teaspoons salt

¼ Cup chopped walnuts

Directions:

Preheat the oven to 350ºf. Lightly coat a 9-by-9-inch baking pan with nonstick cooking spray (if using) or line with parchment paper for oil-free baking.

In a medium bowl, mash the bananas with a fork. Add the maple syrup and vanilla extract and mix well. Add the oats, salt, and walnuts, mixing well.

Transfer the batter to the baking pan and bake for 25 to 30 minutes, until the top is crispy. Cool completely before slicing into 9 bars. Transfer to an airtight storage container or a large plastic bag.

Nutrition (1 bar): calories: 73; fat: 1g; protein: 2g; carbohydrates: 15g; fiber: 2g; sugar: 5g; sodium: 129mg

Lemon Coconut Cilantro Rolls

Preparation time: 30 minutes chill time: 30 minutes

Servings: 16 pieces

Ingredients

½ Cup fresh cilantro, chopped

1 cup sprouts (clover, alfalfa)

1 garlic clove, pressed

2 tablespoons ground brazil nuts or almonds

2 tablespoons flaked coconut

1 tablespoon coconut oil

Pinch cayenne pepper

Pinch sea salt

Pinch freshly ground black pepper

Zest and juice of 1 lemon

2 tablespoons ground flaxseed

1 to 2 tablespoons water

2 whole-wheat wraps, or corn wraps

Directions:

Put everything but the wraps in a food processor and pulse to combine. Or combine the Ingredients in a large bowl. Add the water, if needed, to help the mix come together.

Spread the mixture out over each wrap, roll it up, and place it in the fridge for 30 minutes to set.

Remove the rolls from the fridge and slice each into 8 pieces to serve as appetizers or sides with a soup or stew.

Get the best flavor by buying whole raw brazil nuts or almonds, toasting them lightly in a dry skillet or toaster oven, and then grinding them in a coffee grinder.

Nutrition (1 piece) calories: 66; total fat: 4g; carbs: 6g; fiber: 1g; protein: 2g

Tamari Almonds

Preparation time: 5 minutes

Cooking time: 15 minutes

Servings: 8

Ingredients

1 pound raw almonds

3 tablespoons tamari or soy sauce

2 tablespoons extra-virgin olive oil

1 tablespoon Nutritional yeast

1 to 2 teaspoons chili powder, to taste

Directions: Preheat the oven to 400°f. Line a baking sheet with parchment paper. In a medium bowl, combine the almonds, tamari, and olive oil until well coated. Spread the almonds on the Prepared baking sheet and roast for 10 to 15 minutes, until browned. Cool for 10 minutes, then season with the Nutritional yeast and chili powder. Transfer to a glass jar and close tightly with a lid.

Nutrition: calories: 364; fat: 32g; protein: 13g; carbohydrates: 13g; fiber: 7g; sugar: 3g; sodium: 381mg

Tempeh Taco Bites

Preparation time: 5 minutes

Cooking time: 45 minutes

Servings: 3 dozen

Ingredients

8 ounces tempeh

3 tablespoons soy sauce

2 teaspoons ground cumin

1 teaspoon chili powder

1 teaspoon dried oregano

1 tablespoon olive oil

1/2 cup finely minced onion

2 garlic cloves, minced

Salt and freshly ground black pepper

2 tablespoons tomato paste

1 chipotle chile in adobo, finely minced

1/4 cup hot water or vegetable broth, homemade or store-bought, plus more if needed

36 phyllo pastry cups, thawed

1/2 cup basic guacamole, homemade or store-bought

18 ripe cherry tomatoes, halved

Preparation

In a medium saucepan of simmering water, cook the tempeh for 30 minutes. Drain well, then finely mince and place it in a bowl. Add the soy sauce, cumin, chili powder, and oregano. Mix well and set aside.

In a medium skillet, heat the oil over medium heat. Add the onion, cover, and cook for 5 minutes. Stir in the garlic, then add the tempeh mixture and cook, stirring, for 2 to 3 minutes. Season with salt and pepper to taste. Set aside. In a small bowl, combine the tomato paste, chipotle, and the hot water or broth. Return tempeh mixture to heat and in stir tomato-chile mixture and cook for 10 to 15 minutes, stirring occasionally, until the liquid is absorbed. The mixture should be fairly dry, but if it begins to stick to the pan, add a little more hot water, 1 tablespoon at a time. Taste, adjusting seasonings if necessary. Remove from the heat. To assemble, fill the phyllo cups to the top with the tempeh filling, using about 2 teaspoons of filling in each. Top with a dollop of guacamole and a cherry tomato half and serve.

Mushroom Croustades

Preparation time: 10 minutes

Cooking time: 10 minutes

Servings: 12 croustades

Ingredients

12 thin slices whole-grain bread

1 tablespoon olive oil, plus more for brushing bread

2 medium shallots, chopped

2 garlic cloves, minced

12 ounces white mushrooms, chopped

1/4 cup chopped fresh parsley

1 teaspoon dried thyme

1 tablespoon soy sauce

Preparation

Preheat the oven to 400°f. Using a 3-inch round pastry cutter or a drinking glass, cut a circle from each bread slice. Brush the bread circles with oil and press them firmly but gently into a mini-muffin tin. Bake until the bread is toasted, about 10 minutes.

Meanwhile, in a large skillet, heat the 1 tablespoon oil over medium heat. Add the shallots, garlic, and mushrooms and sauté for 5 minutes to soften the vegetables. Stir in the parsley, thyme, and soy sauce and cook until the liquid is absorbed, about 5 minutes longer. Spoon the mushroom mixture into the croustade cups and return to the oven for 3 to 5 minutes to heat through. Serve warm.

Stuffed Cherry Tomatoes

Preparation time: 15 minutes

Cooking time: 0 minutes

Servings: 6

Ingredients

2 pints cherry tomatoes, tops removed and centers scooped out

2 avocados, mashed

Juice of 1 lemon

½ Red bell pepper, minced

4 green onions (white and green parts), finely minced

1 tablespoon minced fresh tarragon

Pinch of sea salt

Directions:

Place the cherry tomatoes open-side up on a platter. In a small bowl, -combine the avocado, lemon juice, bell pepper, scallions, tarragon, and salt. Stir until well -combined. Scoop into the cherry tomatoes and serve immediately.

Spicy Black Bean Dip

Preparation time: 10 minutes

Cooking time: 0 minutes

Servings: 2 cups

Ingredients

1 (14-ounce) can black beans, drained and rinsed, or 1½ cups cooked

Zest and juice of 1 lime

1 tablespoon tamari, or soy sauce, ¼ Cup water

¼ Cup fresh cilantro, chopped

1 teaspoon ground cumin

Pinch cayenne pepper Directions: Put the beans in a food processor (best choice) or blender, along with the lime zest and juice, tamari, and about ¼ cup of water. Blend until smooth, then blend in the cilantro, cumin, and cayenne. If you don't have a blender or prefer a different consistency, simply transfer it to a bowl once the beans have been puréed and stir in the spices, instead of forcing the blender.

Nutrition (1 cup) calories: 190; total fat: 1g; carbs: 35g; fiber: 12g; protein: 13g

French Onion Pastry Puffs

Preparation time: 10 minutes

Cooking time: 35 minutes - makes 24 puffs

Ingredients

2 tablespoons olive oil

2 medium sweet yellow onions, thinly sliced

1 garlic clove, minced

1 teaspoon chopped fresh rosemary

Salt and freshly ground black pepper

1 tablespoon capers

1 sheet frozen vegan puff pastry, thawed

18 pitted black olives, quartered

Preparation

In a medium skillet, heat the oil over medium heat. Add the onions and garlic, season with rosemary and salt and pepper to taste. Cover and cook until very soft, stirring occasionally, about 20 minutes. Stir in the capers and set aside.

Preheat the oven to 400°f. Roll out the puff pastry and cut into 2- to 3-inch circles using a lightly floured pastry cutter or drinking glass. You should get about 2 dozen circles.

Arrange the pastry circles on baking sheets and top each with a heaping teaspoon of onion mixture, patting down to smooth the top.

Top with 3 olive quarters, arranged decoratively—either like flower petals emanating from the center or parallel to each other like 3 bars.

Bake until pastry is puffed and golden brown, about 15 minutes. Serve hot.

Cheezy Cashew–Roasted Red Pepper Toasts

Preparation time: 15 minutes

Cooking time: 0 minutes

Servings: 16 to 24 toasts

Ingredients

2 jarred roasted red peppers

1 cup unsalted cashews

1/4 cup water

1 tablespoon soy sauce

2 tablespoons chopped green onions

1/4 cup Nutritional yeast

2 tablespoons balsamic vinegar

2 tablespoons olive oil

Preparation

Use canapé or cookie cutters to cut the bread into desired shapes about 2 inches wide. If you don't have a cutter, use a knife to cut the bread into squares, triangles, or rectangles. You should get 2 to 4 pieces out of each slice of bread. Toast the bread and set aside to cool.

Coarsely chop 1 red pepper and set aside. Cut the remaining pepper into thin strips or decorative shapes and set aside for garnish.

In a blender or food processor, grind the cashews to a fine powder. Add the water and soy sauce and process until smooth. Add the chopped red pepper and puree. Add the green onions, Nutritional yeast, vinegar, and oil and process until smooth and well blended.

Spread a spoonful of the pepper mixture onto each of the toasted bread pieces and top decoratively with the reserved pepper strips. Arrange on a platter or tray and serve.

Baked Potato Chips

Preparation time: 10 minutes

Cooking time: 30 minutes

Servings: 4

Ingredients

1 large russet potato

1 teaspoon paprika

½ Teaspoon garlic salt

¼ Teaspoon vegan sugar

¼ Teaspoon onion powder

¼ Teaspoon chipotle powder or chili powder

⅛ Teaspoon salt

⅛ Teaspoon ground mustard

⅛ Teaspoon ground cayenne pepper

1 teaspoon canola oil

⅛ Teaspoon liquid smoke

Directions:

Wash and peel the potato. Cut into thin, 1/10-inch slices (a mandoline slicer or the slicer blade in a food processor is helpful for consistently sized slices).

Fill a large bowl with enough very cold water to cover the potato. Transfer the potato slices to the bowl and soak for 20 minutes.

Preheat the oven to 400°f. Line a baking sheet with parchment paper.

In a small bowl, combine the paprika, garlic salt, sugar, onion powder, chipotle powder, salt, mustard, and cayenne.

Drain and rinse the potato slices and pat dry with a paper towel.

Transfer to a large bowl.

Add the canola oil, liquid smoke, and spice mixture to the bowl. Toss to coat.

Transfer the potatoes to the Prepared baking sheet.

Bake for 15 minutes. Flip the chips over and bake for 15 minutes longer, until browned. Transfer the chips to 4 storage containers or large glass jars. Let cool before closing the lids tightly.

Nutrition: calories: 89; fat: 1g; protein: 2g; carbohydrates: 18g; fiber: 2g; sugar: 1g; sodium: 65mg

Mushrooms Stuffed With Spinach And Walnuts

Preparation time: 10 minutes

Cooking time: 6 minutes

Servings: 4 to 6 servings

Ingredients

2 tablespoons olive oil

8 ounces white mushroom, lightly rinsed, patted dry, and stems reserved

1 garlic clove, minced

1 cup cooked spinach

1 cup finely chopped walnuts

1/2 cup unseasoned dry bread crumbs

Salt and freshly ground black pepper

Preparation

Preheat the oven to 400°f. Lightly oil a large baking pan and set aside. In a large skillet, heat the oil over medium heat. Add the mushroom caps and cook for 2 minutes to soften slightly. Remove from the skillet and set aside.

Chop the mushroom stems and add to the same skillet. Add the garlic and cook over medium heat until softened, about 2 minutes. Stir in the spinach, walnuts, bread crumbs, and salt and pepper to taste. Cook for 2 minutes, stirring well to combine.

Fill the reserved mushroom caps with the stuffing mixture and arrange in the baking pan. Bake until the mushrooms are tender and the filling is hot, about 10 minutes. Serve hot.

Salsa Fresca

Preparation time: 15 minutes

Cooking time: 0 minutes

Servings: 4

Ingredients

3 large heirloom tomatoes or other fresh tomatoes, chopped

½ Red onion, finely chopped

½ Bunch cilantro, chopped

2 garlic cloves, minced

1 jalapeño, minced

Juice of 1 lime, or 1 tablespoon Prepared lime juice

¼ Cup olive oil

Sea salt

Whole-grain tortilla chips, for serving

Directions:

In a small bowl, combine the tomatoes, onion, cilantro, garlic, jalapeño, lime juice, and olive oil and mix well. Allow to sit at room temperature for 15 minutes. Season with salt.

Serve with tortilla chips.

The salsa can be stored in an airtight container in the refrigerator for up to 1 week.

64. Guacamole

Preparation time: 10 minutes

Cooking time: 0 minutes

Servings: 2

Ingredients

2 ripe avocados

2 garlic cloves, pressed

Zest and juice of 1 lime

1 teaspoon ground cumin

Pinch sea salt

Pinch freshly ground black pepper

Pinch cayenne pepper (optional)

Directions:

Mash the avocados in a large bowl. Add the rest of the Ingredients and stir to combine.

Try adding diced tomatoes (cherry are divine), chopped scallions or chives, chopped fresh cilantro or basil, lemon rather than lime, paprika, or whatever you think would taste good!

Nutrition (1 cup) calories: 258; total fat: 22g; carbs: 18g; fiber: 11g; protein: 4g

Veggie Hummus Pinwheels

Preparation time: 10 minutes

Cooking time: 0 minutes

Servings: 3

Ingredients

3 whole-grain, spinach, flour, or gluten-free tortillas

3 large swiss chard leaves

¾ Cup edamame hummus or Prepared hummus

¾ Cup shredded carrots

Directions:

Lay 1 tortilla flat on a cutting board.

Place 1 swiss chard leaf over the tortilla. Spread ¼ cup of hummus over the swiss chard. Spread ¼ cup of carrots over the hummus. Starting at one end of the tortilla, roll tightly toward the opposite side. Slice each roll up into 6 pieces. Place in a single-serving storage container. Repeat with the remaining tortillas and filling and seal the lids.

Nutrition: calories: 254; fat: 8g; protein: 10g; carbohydrates: 39g; fiber: 8g; sugar: 4g; sodium: 488mg

Asian Lettuce Rolls

Preparation time: 15 minutes

Cooking time: 5 minutes

Servings: 4

Ingredients

2 ounces rice noodles, 2 tablespoons chopped thai basil

2 tablespoons chopped cilantro

1 garlic clove, minced, 1 tablespoon minced fresh ginger

Juice of ½ lime, or 2 teaspoons Prepared lime juice

2 tablespoons soy sauce

1 cucumber, julienned

2 carrots, peeled and julienned, 8 leaves butter lettuce

Directions: Cook the rice noodles according to package Preparation. In a small bowl, whisk together the basil, cilantro, garlic, ginger, lime juice, and soy sauce. Toss with the cooked noodles, cucumber, and carrots. Divide the mixture evenly among lettuce leaves and roll. Secure with a toothpick and serve immediately.

Pinto-Pecan Fireballs

Preparation time: 5 minutes

Cooking time: 30 minutes

Servings: about 20 pieces

Ingredients

1-1/2 cups cooked or 1 (15.5-ounce) can pinto beans, drained and rinsed

1/2 cup chopped pecans

1/4 cup minced green onions

1 garlic clove, minced

3 tablespoons wheat gluten flour (vital wheat gluten)

3 tablespoons unseasoned dry bread crumbs

4 tablespoons tabasco or other hot sauce

1/4 teaspoon salt

1/8 teaspoon ground cayenne

1/4 cup vegan margarine

Preparation

Preheat the oven to 350°f. Lightly oil a 9 x 13-inch baking pan and set aside. Blot the drained beans well with a paper towel, pressing out any excess liquid. In a food processor, combine the pinto beans, pecans, green onions, garlic, flour, bread crumbs, 2 tablespoons of the tabasco, salt, and cayenne. Pulse until well combined, leaving some texture. Use your hands to roll the mixture firmly into 1-inch balls.

Place the balls in the Prepared baking pan and bake until nicely browned, about 25 to 30 minutes, turning halfway through.

Meanwhile, in small saucepan, combine the remaining 2 tablespoons tabasco and the margarine and melt over low heat. Pour the sauce over the fireballs and bake 10 minutes longer. Serve immediately.

Chapter 12.   Pre-Workout Recipes

Vegan Chili

Preparation time: 10 minutes

Cooking time: 30 minutes

Servings: 6

Calories: 340

Ingredients

2 tablespoons olive oil

3 cloves of garlic, minced

1 teaspoon chili powder

1 large red onion, thinly sliced

2 celery stalks, finely chopped

1 teaspoon ground cumin

2 medium carrots, peeled and finely chopped

2 red peppers, roughly chopped

Salt and pepper, to taste

28 ounces canned chopped tomatoes

14 ounces red kidney beans, drained and rinsed

3½ ounces split red lentils

14 ounces frozen soy mince

2 tablespoons vegetable stock

Optional:

1 teaspoon miso paste

Large handful fresh coriander, roughly chopped

2 tablespoons balsamic vinegar

To Serve:

Cooked basmati rice

A squeeze of lime juice

Extra chopped coriander

Preparation

Heat olive oil in a large saucepan.

Sauté the onion, garlic, carrot, celery, and peppers for a few minutes on medium heat, until softened.

Add the chili powder, cumin, salt, and pepper and stir.

Toss in the chopped kidney beans, tomatoes, lentils, vegetable stock, and soy mince. Add the extra flavorings, if using.

Simmer for 20 minutes.

Serve with steamed basmati rice, some fresh, torn coriander and a little squeeze of lime juice. Enjoy!

Note: Freezes well. Keep it refrigerated for up to four days.

Nutrition:

Calories 340

Total Fats 6g Saturated Fats 2g

Total Carbohydrates 42g Dietary Fiber 18g

Total Sugar 1g Protein 25g

Sweet Potato Meal Bowls

Cooking time: 25 minutes

Servings: 4

Calories:230

Ingredients

1 large potato, diced into small pieces

3-4 tablespoons olive oil, divided

1 teaspoon seasoning of your choice(or more to taste)

Garlic powder to taste

Salt and pepper to taste

1 can sweet corn, drained

1 can black beans, drained & rinsed

Juice of ½ lime+wedges for serving

½ teaspoon ground cumin

Preparation time: 15 minutes

Preparation

Preheat your oven to 400 degrees F, move the oven rack to the top third of the oven.

Place the cubed sweet potato onto a foil-lined baking sheet. Sprinkle with the seasoning, garlic powder, and salt and pepper, and toss with two to three tablespoon of olive oil. Be sure each piece is coated in oil, but not dripping. Bake for 25 minutes or until tender.

Meanwhile, add the corn, beans, 1 tablespoon of olive oil, lime juice, cumin, salt and pepper (optional) to a small bowl. Toss.

Once your sweet potatoes are ready, equally divide them and the bean/corn mixture between the 4 containers. Add wedge of lime to each container.

Nutrition:

Calories 230 Total Fats 16g Saturated Fats 4g

Total Carbohydrates 64g Dietary Fiber 14g

Total Sugar 12g Protein 12g

Marinated Mushroom Bowls with Wild Rice and Lentils

Preparation time: 10 minutes

Cooking time: 30 minutes

Servings: 4

Calories: 285

Ingredients

Marinated Mushrooms:

¼ cup extra-virgin olive oil

2 tablespoons unseasoned rice vinegar

1 teaspoon low-sodium wheat-free tamari or soy sauce

2 teaspoon dark sesame oil

1 teaspoon chili oil

1 green onion, thinly sliced

1 tablespoon fresh cilantro, chopped

8 ounces crimini mushrooms, thinly sliced

1 teaspoon sesame seeds

Other:

2 cups thinly sliced purple cabbage

1 tablespoon fresh lime juice

Pinch of salt

2 teaspoons low-sodium soy sauce, or (for gluten free) wheat-free tamari, divided

1 cup cooked wild rice

2 cups cooked French lentils

1 cup chopped cucumber

Preparation

To marinate the mushroom, whisk the olive oil, soy sauce, rice vinegar, sesame oil, and chili oil together in a shallow bowl.

Stir in the cilantro, green onion, and sesame seeds. Add in the mushrooms and gently toss in marinade. Cover and let rest 30 minutes.

Place cabbage in a medium-sized bowl and toss with lime juice and a pinch of salt.

Stir one teaspoon of the soy sauce or tamari into the lentils and one teaspoon into the wild rice.

To serve, arrange equal parts of lentils, mushrooms, cabbage, wild rice, and cucumbers in each of the four serving bowls.

Drizzle with the remaining marinade, garnish with chopped cilantro, sliced green onions, and black sesame seeds. Serve with lime wedges.

Nutrition:

Calories 285

Total Fats 10g

Saturated Fats 2.5g

Total Carbohydrates 64g

Dietary Fiber 2g

Total Sugar 16g

Protein 19g

Chirashi Grain Bowl

Preparation time: 5 minutes

Cooking time: 15 minutes

Servings: 3

Calories: 305

Preparation:

Ingredients

7 tablespoons quinoa

4 tablespoons pearl barley

2 ounces lentils

8 broccoli florets

Handful salad leaves

Sesame salad dressing

3 ounces tofu, diced

5 tablespoons edamame, cooked

½ avocado, smashed

5 ounces pickled red cabbage,

1 carrot, thinly sliced

Miso Eggplant:

1 eggplant, diced

1 tablespoon white miso paste

1½ tablespoons mirin

2 teaspoons sugar, 2 teaspoons soy sauce

This protein packed meal with lentils, tofu, quinoa, and edamame combine to offer a full spread of muscle-building amino acids. In a small skillet, sauté the eggplant. Add the mirin, miso, soy sauce, sugar, and a dash of water. Simmer together until soft. Cook grains and the lentils according to the Preparation on the package. Steam broccoli–or any high-protein vegetables of your choice. Dress the leaves and grains and fill a serving bowl. Top with tofu, vegetables, and beans, including one spoonful of the eggplant, arranged in a circle–this is the "chirashi" style. Enjoy it with your chopsticks or fork

Nutrition: Calories 305

Total Fats 14g Saturated Fats 3g Total Carbohydrates 35g

Dietary Fiber 15g Total Sugar 5g Protein 33g

Mushroom Spinach Tofu Wraps

Preparation time: 20 minutes

Cooking time: 20 minutes

Servings: 1

Calories: 305

Ingredients

Cilantro Hummus:

1 14-ounce can chickpeas, rinsed and drained

1 tablespoon tahini

¾ teaspoons salt

1 teaspoon olive oil

Lemon juice of half a lemon

1 tablespoon water+more to thin out

4 stalks of cilantro

Mushroom Pecan Burgers

Preparation time: 15 minutes

Cooking time: 20 minutes

Servings: 5

Ingredients

9 ounces portobello mushrooms

¼ cup red onion, diced

2 cloves garlic, chopped fine or minced

1 cup pecans, diced small

1 15-ounce can chickpeas, drained and patted dry

2 cups instant oats

2 tablespoons hoisin sauce

1 tablespoon tahini or almond butter

Calories: 285

Preparation

Add 2 tablespoons of water to a large skillet. Raise heat to medium high, add the sliced portobello mushrooms. Sauté for 5 minutes.

Add in the onion and sauté for another 5 minutes. Add the garlic and cook 2 more minutes.

Remove from heat, add to a food processor with the pecans and chickpeas. Add the oats (only if they are rolled and not instant).

Process with few pulses to get all the ingredients into small pieces, no chunks.

Transfer to a large mixing bowl and add the tahini and hoisin sauce. If you're using instant oats add that now too.

Mix well. You can also use your hands and work it to work it together well.

Form into 6 patties. You can press them into a round form such as an English Muffin tin round or a pancake ring, about three inches across.

Fry in oil on one side until crispy browned, then carefully flip and brown on the other side.

Serve!

Note: You can also serve these delicious patties on a whole wheat buns with some hoisin sauce on the bottom buns and some vegan mayo on the patty. You can add curly greens and slices of red onion.

Nutrition:

Calories 285

Total Fats 18g

Saturated Fats 1g

Total Carbohydrates 30g

Dietary Fiber 8g

Total Sugar 8g

Protein 13g

Healthy Vegan Tempeh

Preparation time: 30 minutes

Cooking time: 10 minutes

Servings: 2

Calories: 574

Ingredients

Marinated Tempeh:

8 ounces 1 package tempeh

½ cup vegetable broth

1 tablespoon balsamic vinegar

1 tablespoon vegan Worcestershire sauce

1 teaspoon liquid smoke

1 teaspoon onion powder

1 teaspoon smoked paprika

½ teaspoon garlic powder

Other:

4 slices Alvarado's Sprouted Rye Seed Bread

½ heaping cup sauerkraut

¼ cup vegan Russian dressing

Vegan swiss cheese optional

2 tablespoons oil

1 tablespoon vegan butter

Preparation

Slice tempeh in half lengthwise, then slice through the middle into four thin slices.

Combine all the ingredients for the tempeh marinade in a shallow dish. Add the tempeh and marinate for at least 30 minutes.

Heat a large cast-iron skillet on medium heat with two tablespoons oil. Add the tempeh and cook for about 5 minutes per side, until it's dark brown. Once both sides are well-browned, add reserved marinade and allow it to cook off in the skillet. This enables the flavors to seep deeper into the tempeh.

Butter four slices of Sprouted Rye Seed Bread. Place on the skillet and cook for 3-4 minutes, until lightly brown. Flip the bread. On the uncooked sides, add Russian dressing to all slices of bread. Divide the sauerkraut between two slices, top with two pieces cooked tempeh each and one slice of vegan swiss, if using. Add the second slice of bread, cook on each side for about 5 minutes, until the bread is browned and everything is evenly-cooked all the way through.

Remove from the heat and serve immediately.

Nutrition:

Calories 574

Total Fats 33g

Saturated Fats 5g

Total Carbohydrates 47g

Dietary Fiber 4g

Total Sugar 5g

Protein 26g

Broccoli Pesto with Pasta and Cherry Tomatoes

Preparation time: 5 minutes

Cooking time: -20 minutes

Servings: 2

Calories: 239

Ingredients

Broccoli Pesto:

½ cup walnuts

2 heaped cups broccoli florets, cooked

3 tablespoons nutritional yeast

2 cloves of garlic

3 tablespoons olive oil

Black pepper

Salt

½ cup parsley, roughly chopped

Pasta:

1 cup cherry tomatoes, sliced into halves

9 ounces whole-wheat pasta, cooked per the Preparation on the package

1 cup cooked broccoli florets

Preparation

To make the pesto, combine the ingredients in the bowl of a food processor. Season with salt and pepper. Store in one airtight container in refrigerator for up to a week.

Serve with the whole wheat pasta and cherry tomatoes. You can also add more cooked broccoli.

Nutrition:

Calories 239

Total Fats 12g

Saturated Fats 5g

Total Carbohydrates 28g

Dietary Fiber 11g

Total Sugar 9g

Protein 21g

Mongolian Meatless Beef

Preparation time: 10 minutes

Cooking time: 20 minutes

Servings: 6

Calories:324

Ingredients

Mongolian Sauce:

2 teaspoons vegetable oil (grapeseed oil recommended)

⅓ teaspoon red pepper flakes

½ teaspoon minced or grated ginger

3 cloves minced or grated garlic

2 teaspoons cornstarch

⅓ teaspoon Chinese five spice (optional)

½ cup low-sodium soy sauce

½ cup+2 tablespoons coconut sugar (or use a scant ½ cup brown sugar)

2 tablespoons cold water

Crisped Seitan:

1½ tablespoons vegetable oil

1 pound homemade(or store-bought) seitan, cut into 1-inch pieces

Garnish:

Sliced scallions (optional)

Toasted sesame seeds (optional)

Preparation

Sauce:

Heat the vegetable oil in small saucepan over medium heat. Add ginger and garlic, stirring constantly. After 30 seconds, add the five spice (if using) and red pepper flakes, cook for 30-60 seconds more, until fragrant.

Add soy sauce and coconut sugar, stir well. Reduce the heat to a medium-low, let simmer until coconut sugar dissolves and it is slightly reduced, about 5-7 minutes, stirring occasionally.

Whisk cornstarch and cold water together then add it to pan and stir. Cook for 2-3 more minutes, until sauce becomes glossy and thickened slightly. Reduce heat to the lowest setting, keep simmering gently until it's ready to add to the seitan.

Seitan:

In your skillet, heat the oil over medium-high heat. Add seitan and cook, stirring frequently for 4-5 minutes or until slightly browned and crisped around edges.

Reduce heat to low and add the sauce. Stir to coat all the seitan pieces, continue cooking until sauce has adhered to the seitan. Remove from the heat and serve hot with rice and vegetables of your choice. Garnish with scallions and sesame seeds if desired.

Nutrition:

Calories 324

Total Fats 8g

Saturated Fats 1g

Total Carbohydrates 33g

Dietary Fiber 3g

Total Sugar 19g

Protein 29g

Mexican Lentil Soup

Preparation time: 15 minutes

Cooking time: 30 minutes

Servings: 4

Calories: 235

Ingredients

2 tablespoons extra virgin olive oil

1 yellow onion, diced

1 red bell pepper, diced

2 carrots, peeled and diced

2 celery stalks, diced

3 cloves garlic, minced

1 tablespoon cumin

¼ teaspoon smoked paprika

1 teaspoon oregano

2 cups diced tomatoes and the juices

2 (4-ounce) cans diced green chilies

2 cups green lentils, rinsed and picked over

8 cups vegetable broth

½ teaspoon salt

Dash hot sauce, plus more for serving (adjust to taste)

Fresh cilantro, for garnish

1 avocado, peeled, pitted, and diced

Directions:

Heat olive oil in large-sized pot over medium heat. Add carrots, onion, celery, and bell pepper. Sauté until it starts to soften, about 5 minutes. Add the garlic, paprika, cumin, and oregano and sauté another minute. Add the tomatoes, lentils, chilies, broth, and salt. Bring to simmer. Simmer with the lid tilted until the lentils are tender, about 30-40 minutes. Season to taste with salt and pepper. Serve the Mexican Lentil Soup topped with fresh avocado, cilantro, and a few dashes of hot sauce.

Nutrition: Calories 235 Total Fats 9g Saturated Fats 1g

Total Carbohydrates 32g Dietary Fiber 10g Total Sugar 13g Protein 12g

Chapter 13.   Post-Workout Recipes

Farro Protein Bowl

Servings: 2

Preparation time: 10 minutes

Cooking time: 25 minutes

Ingredients:

1/2 cup farro, uncooked

4 ounces smoky tempeh strips

1 cup diced sweet potatoes

2 cups mixed greens

12 ounces cooked chickpeas

1 cup diced carrots

1/3 teaspoon ground black pepper

2/3 teaspoon salt

2 tablespoons roasted almonds

2 teaspoons olive oil, divided

1/4 cup hummus

1 1/4 cups water

4 lemon, cut into wedges

Directions:

Switch on the oven, then set it to 375 degrees F and let it preheat.

Meanwhile, take a medium bowl, place sweet potato and carrots in it, drizzle with 1 teaspoon oil, season with half of each salt and black pepper, toss until mixed and then spread the vegetables on a third of a large baking sheet.

Add chickpeas into the same bowl, drizzle with the remaining oil, season with remaining salt and black pepper, toss until well coated and spread the chickpeas on second-third of the baking sheet. Arrange tempeh strips on the remaining space of the baking sheet and then roast it, chickpeas and vegetables for 30 minutes, stirring vegetables and flipping tempeh strips halfway. Meanwhile, cook the farro beans and for this, take a medium pot, place it over medium-high heat, add farro grains in it, stir in a pinch of salt, pour in water and bring to a boil. Then cover the pot with a lid, switch heat to medium-low level and cook for 25 minutes until grains have turned soft. When farro has cooked, distribute evenly between two bowls, top with roasted tempeh, chickpeas, sweet potatoes, and hummus, sprinkle with almonds, and then serve with lemon wedges. Serve straight away.

Teriyaki Tofu with Quinoa

Servings: 4

Preparation time: 10 minutes

Cooking time: 20 minutes

Ingredients:

For the Tofu:

2 cups diced asparagus

14 ounces tofu, firm, pressed, ½-inch cubed

2 tablespoons chopped green onions

2 teaspoons red chili paste

1 tablespoon soy sauce

2 teaspoons olive oil

For the Sauce:

2 tablespoons minced garlic

2 teaspoons corn starch

1/2 tablespoon grated ginger

1/4 cup coconut sugar

1 tablespoon sesame oil

3 tablespoons soy sauce

1 ½ tablespoon rice vinegar

1/2 cup water

For Serving:

4 cups cooked quinoa

Directions: Prepare the tofu and for this, take a medium skillet pan, place it over medium-high heat, add 1 teaspoon of olive oil and when hot, add tofu pieces and then cook for 5 minutes until golden brown on all sides. Then transfer tofu pieces to a bowl, drizzle with soy sauce, toss until coated, and set aside until required. Prepare the sauce and for this, take a small bowl, place all of its ingredients in it and whisk until combined. Return skillet pan over medium-high heat, add remaining oil and when hot, add asparagus and then cook for 5 to 7 minutes until tender-crisp. Return tofu pieces into the pan, drizzle with Prepared sauce, toss until well combined, then switch heat to medium level and cook for 3 to 4 minutes until the sauce has thickened. Add green onions and red chili paste, stir until mixed, and then remove the pan from heat. Remove pan from heat, then distribute quinoa among serving bowls, top with tofu and vegetables, and serve.

Buddha Bowl

Servings: 2

Preparation time: 10 minutes

Cooking time: 20 minutes

Ingredients:

For the Bowl:

8 ounces tofu, firm, pressed,

1 ½ cups cooked quinoa

1 medium white onion, peeled, sliced

1 cup spinach

1 medium sweet potato, peeled, cubed

¼ cup shredded carrots

1 avocado, pitted, diced

1 cup cooked chickpeas

1 teaspoon minced garlic

1 teaspoon garlic powder

1 teaspoon ground black pepper

1 teaspoon salt

1 teaspoon red chili powder

2 tablespoons olive oil

1 lemon, juiced

For the Marinade:

½ teaspoon salt

1 teaspoon hot sauce

1 teaspoon paprika

2 teaspoons dried thyme

2 tablespoons olive oil

½ teaspoon sesame oil

Directions:

Switch on the oven, then set it to 400 degrees F and let it preheat.

Prepare the bowl and for this, take a small bowl, place all of its ingredients in it and then whisk until combined.

Cut tofu into ½-inch cubes, place them in a container, pour in Prepared marinade, toss until well coated, and then marinate tofu pieces for 30 minutes.

Take a large baking sheet, place onion, sweet potato and garlic in it, drizzle with 1 tablespoon oil, season with half of each black pepper and salt, toss until combined, and then bake for 20 minutes until cooked.

Prepare the chickpeas and for this, take a medium bowl, add chickpeas in it, add remaining salt and black pepper, garlic powder and chili powder and stir until combined.

Take a medium skillet pan, place it over medium heat, add remaining oil and when hot, add chickpeas in it and cook for 10 minutes until done.

Transfer chickpeas to a plate, add marinated tofu pieces in it and cook for 10 minutes per side until golden brown, set aside until required.

When vegetables have roasted, take a medium-large bowl, add tofu, quinoa, chickpeas, spinach, sweet potatoes, avocado, onion, and carrots, drizzle with lemon juice and toss until just mixed. Serve straight away.

Chinese Tofu and Broccoli

Servings: 4

Preparation time: 10 minutes

Cooking time: 20 minutes

Ingredients:

3 cups broccoli florets

14 ounces tofu, firm, pressed, ½-inch cubed

1 teaspoon minced garlic

1 teaspoon grated ginger

1 tablespoon cornstarch

2 tablespoons agave syrup

1 tablespoon rice vinegar

1 teaspoon olive oil

¼ cup of soy sauce

1 ½ teaspoons sesame oil, divided

1 tablespoon water

3 tablespoons vegetable broth

1 teaspoon toasted sesame seeds and more for serving

4 tablespoons sliced scallions

2 cups cooked white rice

Directions:

Take a large skillet pan, place it over medium-high heat, add olive oil and 1 teaspoon sesame oil, and when hot, add tofu pieces and cook for 4 minutes per side until golden brown.

When done, transfer the tofu pieces to a plate, add broccoli florets to the pan, pour in the broth, switch heat to medium-low level and cook for 5 minutes until broccoli has steamed, covering the pan.

Then switch heat to medium-high level, stir in ginger, garlic, and remaining sesame oil and cook for 1 minute.

Stir together cornstarch and water until smooth, add to the pan along with sesame seeds, vinegar, agave syrup, and soy sauce, stir until mixed and cook for 2 minutes until the sauce has thickened.

Return tofu pieces to the skillet pan, toss until well coated with the sauce and then remove the pan from heat.   Distribute cooked rice among bowls, top with tofu and broccoli, sprinkle with scallion and sesame seeds and then serve.

Peanut Butter Tempeh with Rice

Servings: 4

Preparation time: 3 hours and 10 minutes

Cooking time: 30 minutes

Ingredients:

6.5 ounces brown rice, cooked

22 ounces Tempeh, 1-inch cubed

Olive oil as needed

For the Sauce:

4 teaspoons coconut sugar

2 tablespoons grated ginger

1 tablespoon minced garlic

2 tablespoons red chili sauce

4 tablespoons soy sauce

2 teaspoons rice vinegar

4 tablespoons peanut butter

6 tablespoons water

For the Cabbage:

1 lime, juiced

5 ounces purple cabbage, sliced

3 teaspoons sesame oil

2 teaspoons honey

For Garnish:

4 tablespoons chopped Green onion

Directions: Prepare the sauce and for this, take a large bowl, place all of its ingredients in it and whisk until combined. Add tempeh pieces into the peanut butter sauce, toss until well coated, then place the bowl in the refrigerator and let it marinate for a minimum of 3 hours. When tofu is almost marinated, switch on the oven, then set the temperature to 375 degrees F and let it preheat. Transfer marinated tempeh pieces to a baking sheet, spray with olive oil and then bake for 30 minutes until nicely browned and cooked, turning halfway. Meanwhile, Prepare the cabbage and for this, take a medium bowl, place all of its ingredients in it and toss until combined, set aside until required. When tempeh has baked, distribute cabbage, rice and tempeh pieces evenly among bowls, drizzle with the marinade sauce, garnish with green onions and then serve.

Soy Beans and Puy lentil Salad

Servings: 4

Preparation time: 10 minutes

Cooking time: 25 minutes

Ingredients:

For the Salad:

8 ounces of broccoli florets, chopped

1 red chili, deseeded, sliced

8 ounces of Puy lentils, uncooked

5 ounces sugar snap peas

5 ounces frozen soya bean, thawed

4 ¼ cups vegetable stock, hot

For the Dressing:

1-inch piece of ginger, grated

½ teaspoon minced garlic

1 lemon, juiced

1 tablespoon honey

3 tablespoons soy sauce

2 tablespoons sesame oil

Directions:

Take a large pot, place it over medium-high heat, pour in the stock, bring it to a boil, then add lentils and cook for 15 minutes until tender.

Drain the cooked lentils, transfer them to a large bowl and set aside until required.

Drain the pot, fill it half-full with water, bring it to a boil, then add broccoli florets and cook for 1 minute.

Add soya beans and peas, continue cooking for 1 minute, then drain these vegetables, rinse under cold water and transfer them to the bowl containing lentils.

Prepare the dressing and for this, take a small bowl, place all of its ingredients in it and whisk until combined.

Pour the dressing over lentil and vegetable mixture, add red chili, and stir until well mixed.

Serve straight away.

Tofu and Greens Stir-Fry with Cashews

Servings: 4

Preparation time: 5 minutes

Cooking time: 8 minutes

Ingredients:

5 ounces soya bean

1 bunch of spring onions, sliced

2 heads of bok choi, quartered, 1 head broccoli, cut into florets

10 ounces of marinated tofu pieces, 1 red chili, deseeded, sliced

2 teaspoons minced garlic, 1 tablespoon soy sauce

1 ½ tablespoon hoisin sauce, 1 tablespoon olive oil

1 ½ tablespoon roasted cashew

Directions: Take a large skillet pan, place it over high heat, add oil and when hot, add broccoli florets and cook for 5 minutes until tender. Stir in red chili and garlic, continue cooking for 1 minute, add soya beans, spring onions, tofu, and bok choi, and stir-fry for 3 minutes. Drizzle with soy sauce and hoisin sauce, sprinkle with nuts, cook for 1 minute until hot and then serve.

Spiced Crusted Tofu with Salad

Servings: 2

Preparation time: 10 minutes

Cooking time: 15 minutes

Ingredients:

For the Tofu:

8 ounces of tofu, firmed, pressed, 1-inch cubed

4 ounces sugar snap peas

3 kumquats, sliced

4 radishes, sliced

8 ounces broccoli florets

2 spring onions, chopped

1 tablespoon Japanese spice mix

2 tablespoons sesame seeds

½ tablespoon cornflour

1 tablespoon sesame oil

1 tablespoon olive oil

For the Dressing:

1 small shallot, diced

1 teaspoon grated ginger

1 tablespoon lime juice

1 teaspoon caster sugar

2 tablespoons soy sauce

1 tablespoon grapefruit juice

Directions: Prepare the dressing and for this, take a small bowl, place all of its ingredients in it and then stir until well combined.   Prepare the tofu and for this, take a small bowl, add cornflour in it, stir in Japanese spice mix and sesame seeds, and then sprinkle this mixture on all sides of tofu pieces until evenly coated.   Take a large pot, fill it half full with water, place it over high heat, bring it to a boil, then switch heat to medium level, add peas and broccoli and boil for 3 minutes until tender-crisp. While water comes to a boil, take a large skillet pan, place it over medium heat, add oil and when hot, add tofu pieces and cook for 5 minutes until nicely browned. When Vegetables have cooked to the desired level, distribute them evenly between two bowls, top with cooked tofu, and then drizzle with Prepared dressing. Top with spring onions, radishes, and kumquats and then serve.

Sprouts with Green Beans and Nuts

Servings: 4

Preparation time: 5 minutes

Cooking time: 12 minutes

Ingredients:

21 ounces Brussels sprouts, quartered

21 ounces green beans

4 tablespoons toasted pine nuts

1 lemon, juiced, zested

1 tablespoon olive oil

Directions:

Take a large pot, fill it half full with water, place it over high heat, bring it to a boil, then switch heat to medium level, add beans and sprouts, and boil for 3 minutes until tender-crisp and when done, drain the beans and sprouts. Take a large skillet pan, place it medium heat, add oil and when hot, add nuts and lemon zest and cook for 30 seconds. Then add sprouts and green beans, stir-fry them for 4 minutes, then season with black pepper and salt and drizzle with lemon juice. Remove pan from heat and then serve.

Tofu with Noodles

Servings: 2

Preparation time: 25 minutes

Cooking time: 25 minutes

Ingredients:

8 ounces of tofu, firm, pressed, 1-inch cubed

6 ounces dried soba noodles, cooked

½ of a large cucumber

¼ teaspoon salt

2 tablespoons caster sugar

2 tablespoons sesame seeds

4 tablespoons white miso paste

½ cup of rice wine vinegar

2 tablespoons maple syrup

½ cup olive oil

¼ cup of water

2 spring onions, shredded

Directions:

Prepare the noodles, and for this, use a vegetable peeler to cut ribbons from the cucumber and place them in a bowl.

Take a small saucepan, place it over medium heat, add sugar, salt, vinegar, and water, stir until combined, and cook for 5 minutes until the sugar has dissolved.

Pour this mixture over cucumber ribbons, then place the bowl in the refrigerator and leave it to pickle.

Prepare the tofu and for this, take a large skillet pan, add 1 tablespoon oil in it and when hot, add tofu pieces and cook for 7 to 10 minutes until nicely golden brown on all sides. When done, transfer the tofu pieces to a plate lined with kitchen towels and then set aside until required. Take a small bowl, add honey and miso paste in it, whisk until combined, and then brush this mixture on tofu pieces until evenly coated. When cucumber ribbons have pickles, drain them, and then rinse them well under cold water. Return the skillet pan over medium heat and when hot, add remaining oil, cucumber ribbons, remaining honey-miso mixture and 1 tablespoon of the cucumber pickling liquid and continue cooking for 3 minutes until warm. When done, divide soba noodles between bowls, then top evenly with tofu and cucumber ribbons, sprinkle with green onions, and then serve.

Black Bean and Seitan Stir-Fry

Servings: 4

Preparation time: 15 minutes

Cooking time: 25 minutes

Ingredients:

For the Sauce:

1 red chili, chopped

12 ounces cooked black beans

1 tablespoon minced garlic

1 teaspoon Chinese five-spice powder

2.5 ounces brown sugar

2 tablespoons rice vinegar

2 tablespoons soy sauce

1 tablespoon peanut butter

¼ cup of water

For the Stir-Fry:

12 ounces marinated seitan pieces

2 spring onions, sliced

10 ounces bok choi, chopped

1 red pepper, sliced

1 tablespoon cornflour

3 tablespoons olive oil

2 cups cooked brown rice

Directions:

Prepare the sauce, and for this, place half of the black beans in a food processor, then add remaining ingredients and pulse for 2 minutes until smooth.

Tip the sauce in a medium saucepan, place it over medium heat, cook for 5 minutes until thickened, and then set aside until required.

Drain the marinated seitan, pat dries the seitan pieces with kitchen towels, then dredge seitan into cornflour and set aside until required.

Take a large skillet pan, place it over high heat, add 1 teaspoon oil and when hot, add seitan pieces and fry them for 5 minutes until edges have turned golden brown.

When done, transfer seitan pieces to a plate and set aside until required.

Add 1 teaspoon oil into the skillet pan, add shallots, cook for 4 minutes until softened, then add red pepper, spring onion, bok choi, and remaining black beans, stir until mixed and cook for 4 minutes.

Return seitan pieces into the pan, pour in the Prepared sauce, toss until mixed, and cook for 1 minute until hot.

Serve seitan and vegetables over brown rice.

Conclusion

"The latest suggestions explain not exactly what number of grams of protein you ought to eat, yet in addition how those grams are beat for the duration of the day," Pojednic says.

"Researchers are thinking now that there's just a specific measure of protein your muscles can take-up and use in one sitting. On the off chance that you flood your framework with amino acids, sooner or later they're somewhat squandered."

Intend to get 0.25 and 0.4 grams of protein per kilogram of body weight per feast. Or on the other hand, to place it way less difficult, space out your protein more than 3 or 4 dinners per day, not only at the same time in a uber smoothie.

The other science-sponsored tip is to ensure you're eating 20-30 grams of protein inside 30 minutes (as long as an hour is presumably fine) of Preparation. " The science is somewhat muddier for eating previously and during Preparation. Pojednic says to go with your inclination, and how much nourishment you need in your stomach related tract while you're doing overwhelming squats. Over-burdening your G.I. framework is especially simple for veggie lovers, whose nourishments contain such a lot of fiber. You can get a belly throb from eating a serving of mixed greens before Preparation, on the grounds that all the blood is "shunted away" from your stomach related organs for, state, your quads. On the off chance that you would prefer not to eat before Preparation, yet need to ensure you have enough sugar in your framework to capitalize on your exercise, Pojednic suggests organic product juice.

Be that as it may, the most urgent parts of picking up muscle have nothing to do with being veggie lover.

It's not tied in with getting enough amino acids. You must eat enough calories to increase mass, and you must train hard. Farris, who went plant-situated in November 2014 (between Olympics appearances), is a world-class competitor who happens to be veggie lover—and he doesn't follow his protein by any stretch of the imagination. All things considered, he had the option to "make a few additions and, all the more critically, remain solid." He says a vegetarian diet has let him recoup quicker. "On the off chance that you can do that, you can accomplish more work. You can pummel your body more. Essentially, simply train."

(It's important that piece of the explanation Farris had no second thoughts about changing his eating routine while in a high purpose of his profession was on the grounds that he spent his prime lifting years (19-22) picking up quality without solid access to any kind of nourishment whatsoever. "In the event that I could lift and do everything when I didn't approach customary dinners, how was I going to get more fragile eating enough nourishment however changing out the fixings?")

"A major issue for vegetarians is that they can without much of a stretch under eat," Zinchenko says. "Particularly dynamic individuals who eat a great deal of entire nourishments. Without calories, your body can't make muscle."

"The primary concern is high-volume weight Preparation and getting satisfactory supplements," David says. "That is it. There are no alternate ways. The harder you hit it, the more you feed it, the more it will develop." (I accept we were discussing butts now in the discussion.)

"Clearly diet is going to give you that minor push toward the end, yet the Preparation and the commitment is actually what's going issue in the long haul for significant level competitors," Polojic says.

Goodness, and for what it's worth, we painfully need more research on veggie lovers. "Indeed, even the investigations that analyze veggie lover protein powders are not done on vegetarians," Zinchenko says. "In the event that there is someone who might want to give cash to contemplate veggie lover muscle development, I would be glad to run the investigation."

The generalization of the powerless, thin veggie lover has become so all inclusive that the vast majority would make some hard memories accepting any individual of noteworthy size or quality didn't eat meat or other creature items. This is on the grounds that we've been adapted to accept that you have to eat bunches of creature protein to assemble muscle and quality, and that protein extremely just originates from creature nourishments.

Obviously just one of those two convictions is in reality valid, as any individual who has ever observed a (herbivorous) silverback gorilla can without much of a stretch derive.

The vast majority, notwithstanding, assume athlete sare progressively similar to lions, requiring meat or some type of creature protein at each dinner to get large and solid. As talked about in What About Protein? there are numerous purposes behind how this fantasy turned out to be so imbued in the mainstream society, yet actually from the flower child culture of the 60s until decently as of late, a great deal of the individuals who followed a plant-based eating regimen were really thin. This is halfway in light of the fact that, for a very long while, a great many athletes who picked meat/creature free eating regimens did so exclusively for moral, ecological or wellbeing reasons, and didn't generally think about having large muscles. Furthermore, the individuals who cared frequently did not have the fundamental healthful understanding important to assemble muscle and quality eating plants.

As confirm in The Game Changers, the entirety of that has changed. The age of the frail, celery-crunching vegetarian is finished. Indeed, even Arnold Schwarzenegger — the back up parent of muscle and quality — is presently encouraging individuals to "simply chill it with the meat", recognizing that there is no motivation behind why eating a plant-based eating regimen should represent any boundaries to getting enormous and solid, and that doing so may much offer some noteworthy focal points.

Building muscle and quality is in reality quite basic from a physiological perspective: turn out reliably and eat heaps of nourishment. On the off chance that you train hard however don't eat enough — or eat loads of nourishment yet don't Prepare enough — you most likely won't increase a lot of muscle or get a lot more grounded. This applies to everybody, regardless of whether you eat meat or not.

For amateur lifters, eating "bunches of nourishment" signifies devouring 10-20% a larger number of calories than required for every day upkeep, and for further developed lifters, 5-10% progressively.

An incredible aspect regarding plant-based nourishment is that, by volume, it normally contains less calories than creature-based food sources, enabling us to eat increasingly all out nourishment and feel more full, without essentially increasing more muscle versus fat. You can discover increasingly about that in Getting and Staying Lean. For individuals whose top need is to pick up muscle and quality, individuals on a plant-put together eating regimen need to center with respect to plant-based nourishments that have higher caloric thickness than state, lettuce. As a rule, this implies ensuring that suppers and bites incorporate heavy measures of grains, beans, tofu and tempeh, meat and dairy choices, nuts and nut spreads, seeds, avocados, dried natural product, and so on., notwithstanding leafy foods. Those less worried about eating essentially entire nourishments can likewise incorporate plant-based meats, plant-based protein powders, plant-based protein/vitality bars — whatever it takes to get hit the fundamental caloric excess.

www.ingramcontent.com/pod-product-compliance
Lightning Source LLC
Chambersburg PA
CBHW081406080526
44589CB00016B/2485